How to modify

LAND ROVER

DISCOVERY, DEFENDER & RANGE ROVER

for high performance & serious off-road action

VELOCE PUBLISHING
THE PUBLISHER OF FINE AUTOMOTIVE BOOKS

Land Rover Discovery 1989 to 1998, Land Rover 90, 110 and Defender 1983 to 2010, Range Rover 1970 to 1995

Also includes information on servicing, repair, racing, expeditions and trekking, plus a buyers' guide

Contents

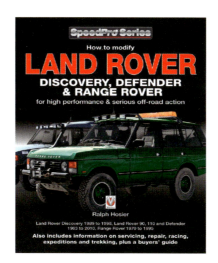

SpeedPro Series

How to modify

LAND ROVER

DISCOVERY, DEFENDER & RANGE ROVER

for high performance & serious off-road action

Ralph Hosier

Land Rover Discovery 1989 to 1998, Land Rover 90, 110 and Defender
1983 to 2010, Range Rover 1970 to 1995

**Also includes information on servicing, repair, racing,
expeditions and trekking, plus a buyers' guide**

Other great books from Veloce –

Speedpro Series
4-cylinder Engine – How to Blueprint & Build a Short Block For High Performance (Hammill)
Camshafts – How to Choose & Time Them For Maximum Power (Hammill)
Competition Car Datalogging Manual, The (Templeman)
Cylinder Heads – How to Build, Modify & Power Tune Updated & Revised Edition (Burgess & Gollan)
Distributor-type Ignition Systems – How to Build & Power Tune New 3rd Edition (Hammill)
Fast Road Car – How to Plan and Build Revised & Updated Colour New Edition (Stapleton)
Ford SOHC 'Pinto' & Sierra Cosworth DOHC Engines – How to Power Tune Updated & Enlarged Edition (Hammill)
Ford V8 – How to Power Tune Small Block Engines (Hammill)
Holley Carburetors – How to Build & Power Tune Revised & Updated Edition (Hammill)
Jaguar XK Engines – How to Power Tune Revised & Updated Colour Edition (Hammill)
Motorsport – Getting Started in (Collins)
Rover V8 Engines – How to Power Tune (Hammill)
Secrets of Speed – Today's techniques for 4-stroke engine blueprinting & tuning (Swager)
Sportscar & Kitcar Suspension & Brakes – How to Build & Modify Revised 3rd Edition (Hammill)
SU Carburettor High-performance Manual (Hammill)
Successful Low-Cost Rally Car, How to Build a (Young)
Suzuki 4x4 – How to Modify For Serious Off-road Action (Richardson)
V8 Engine – How to Build a Short Block For High Performance (Hammill)
Weber DCOE, & Dellorto DHLA Carburetors – How to Build & Power Tune 3rd Edition (Hammill)

General
Daily Mirror 1970 World Cup Rally 40, The (Robson)
Drive on the Wild Side, A – 20 Extreme Driving Adventures From Around the World (Weaver)
Dune Buggy, Building A – The Essential Manual (Shakespeare)
Dune Buggy Files (Hale)
Dune Buggy Handbook (Hale)
Ford F100/F150 Pick-up 1948-1996 (Ackerson)
Ford F150 Pick-up 1997-2005 (Ackerson)
Jaguar, The Rise of (Price)
Jaguar XJ 220 – The Inside Story (Moreton)
Jaguar XJ-S (Long)
Jeep CJ (Ackerson)

Jeep Wrangler (Ackerson)
Land Rover Series III Reborn (Porter)
Land Rover, The Half-ton Military (Cook)
Peking to Paris 2007 (Young)
Roads with a View – England's greatest views and how to find them by road (Corfield)
Roads With a View – Wales' greatest views and how to find them by road (Corfield)

From Veloce Publishing's new imprints:

Battle Cry!
Soviet General & field rank officer uniforms: 1955 to 1991 (Streather)
Red & Soviet military & paramilitary services: female uniforms 1941-1991 (Streather)

Hubble & Hattie
Animal Grief – how animals mourn for each other (Alderton)
Clever Dog! (O'Meara)
Complete Dog Massage Manual, The – Gentle Dog Care (Robertson)
Dinner with Rover (Paton-Ayre)
Dog Cookies (Schops)
Dog Games – stimulating play to entertain your dog and you (Blenski)
Dogs on wheels (Mort)
Dog Relax – Relaxed dogs, relaxed owners (Pilguj)
Exercising your puppy: a gentle & natural approach – Gentle Dog Care (Robertson)
Fun and games for cats (Seidl)
Know Your Dog – The guide to a beautiful relationship (Birmelin)
Living with an Older Dog – Gentle Dog Care (Alderton & Hall)
My dog has cruciate ligament injury – but lives life to the full! (Häusler)
My dog has hip dysplasia – but lives life to the full! (Häusler)
My dog is blind – but lives life to the full! (Horsky)
My dog is deaf – but lives life to the full! (Willms)
Smellorama – nose games for dogs (Theby)
Swim to Recovery: Canine hydrotherapy healing (Wong)
Waggy Tails & Wheelchairs (Epp)
Walkin' the dog – motorway walks for dogs and drivers (Rees)
Winston … the dog who changed my life (Klute)
You and Your Border Terrier – The Essential Guide (Alderton)
You and Your Cockapoo – The Essential Guide (Alderton)

www.veloce.co.uk

First published in February 2011 by Veloce Publishing Limited, Veloce House, Parkway Farm Business Park, Middle Farm Way, Poundbury, Dorchester, Dorset, DT1 3AR, England.
Fax 01305 250479/e-mail info@veloce.co.uk/web www.veloce.co.uk or www.velocebooks.com.

ISBN: 978-1-845843-15-1 UPC: 6-36847-04315-5

SPEEDPRO SERIES

978-1-845840-05-1

978-1-845840-06-8

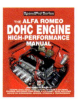
978-1-845840-19-8

978-1-845840-21-1

978-1-845840-23-5 | 978-1-845840-45-7

978-1-845840-73-0

978-1-845841-23-2

978-1-845841-42-3

978-1-845841-62-1

978-1-845841-86-7 | 978-1-845841-87-4

978-1-845842-07-9

978-1-845842-08-6

978-1-845842-24-6

978-1-845842-62-8

978-1-845842-66-6

978-1-845842-97-0

978-1-845843-15-1

978-1-845843-55-7

978-1-874105-70-1

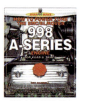
978-1-901295-26-9

978-1-903706-17-6

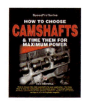
978-1-903706-59-6

978-1-903706-68-8

978-1-903706-70-1

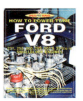
978-1-903706-72-5

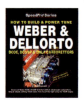
978-1-903706-75-6

978-1-903706-76-3

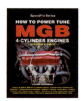
978-1-903706-77-0

978-1-903706-78-7

978-1-903706-80-0

978-1-903706-92-3

978-1-903706-94-7

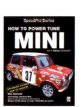
978-1-903706-99-2

978-1-904788-22-5

978-1-904788-78-2

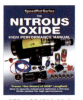
978-1-904788-84-3

978-1-904788-89-8

978-1-904788-91-1

978-1-904788-93-5

Introduction & acknowledgements

To Diana and Peter, and all the adventures yet to come

A Defender 90 Challenge truck built by Devon 4x4 – the ultimate 'go anywhere' vehicle? (Courtesy Devon 4x4)

INTRODUCTION

The coil-sprung Land Rover chassis that underpins the classic Range Rover, Discovery Mk1, and Defender models makes one of the best off-road vehicles in the world, yet also manages the neat trick of having remarkably good road manners. This combination of comfort and capability was instrumental in the 4x4 revolution that has taken place over the last 40 years.

From the mean streets of the city to the rough tracks of the jungle, it's amazing how versatile this simple yet well-thought-out chassis has proven to be. It has competed in top level motorsport successfully, been used in exploration of the planets most hostile terrain, and also been subject to luxurious conversions that rival Rolls-Royce for opulence.

This book is dedicated to those who recognise this great feat, and would like to know a bit more, maybe stretch the vehicles abilities and see what else it can do.

So whether you just want to know

7

how to keep your standard car in good health, or see what is involved with racing in the Dakar Rally, I hope you will find something here to let you enjoy your Land Rover that little bit more.

ACKNOWLEDGEMENTS

Thanks to all the companies who took time to answer my long-winded questions and let me invade busy workshops with my camera. In particular, a great debt of thanks is owed to Drew Bowler, Devon 4x4, and Tomcat Motorsport which have all been very helpful and enthusiastic about its Land Rovers.

Also thanks to the Discovery Owners Club who let me photograph its cars on Pendine beach whilst it did sterling work supporting the World Land Speed Record run from Runningblade.

Many of my friends in the Deranged Off-road Club supplied pictures and stories used in this book – a fantastic group of people and a superb example of a small local off-road club.

Writing a book is a big job that requires lots of time, and quite a lot of tea. It also requires the support and understanding of my family, specifically Diana, who has encouraged, cajoled, and proofread. The biggest thanks go to her.

Top: The coil-sprung Land Rovers make superb adventure vehicles. Here, a club tour up a glacier in the mountains stops for some tea.

Above: Even unmodified the Land Rovers are immensely capable – built for this kind of rough track.

Right: But when highly modified, they become world-beating race machines. Here, a Bowler powers through the desert on the Dakar Rally. (Courtesy Drew Bowler)

Chapter 1
History

The story of the Range Rover began almost as soon as the first Land Rover hit the production line in 1948. The idea of a rugged yet more refined estate car inspired by the agricultural off-roader made sense, even then.

It spawned an evaluation prototype in the early '50s called the Road Rover, which was made from a great number of Land Rover parts including front wings, extended bonnet, bulkhead and screen,

How it all started; the original Land Rover came out in 1948, but planning for a luxury version began immediately.

door shells, and load bed, but based on a Rover P4 chassis. To make it more friendly, it sported a traditional car-type grille and interior luxuries. Curiously, despite the Land Rover connection, it was only two-wheel drive.

Numerous variations on the theme were tried, and in 1959 a more handsome Road Rover prototype was made. This looked like a standard estate car of the time, but again nothing much happened for a few more years – or so it seemed.

Behind closed doors work continued, however, and the Range Rover as we know it was being conceived. In 1966, Charles Spencer King and Gordon Bashford combined the idea of a luxury Land Rover with Rover's recently acquired 3.5-litre alloy V8 engine on an 100in ladder chassis. Another prototype was born in 1967, but this time it was part of a plan that would lead to production cars in just a few years.

By the end of 1969, the valiant

The Range Rover arrived in 1970, originally only in two-door form. This model has the Webasto sunroof.

prototypes had served their purpose and were retired. The production line needed to be tested, and a run of only 25 cars was made, with number plates YVB151H to YVB175H. In an attempt to maintain some secrecy, these cars were labelled 'Velar,' possibly from the Latin for veil. Some were used in the press launch; originally planned to be in the exotic location of North Africa, but in the end they went for the arguably equally exotic Meudon Hotel in Cornwall.

Interestingly, chassis number 2 was turned into a six-wheel Carmichael fire tender and used at Cambridge airport.

So, in 1970 on the 17th of June the Range Rover was officially launched, and immediately started winning awards. It looked good and drove superbly. At a shade over 1700kg and with 136bhp it made very good progress, and was remarkably nimble for an estate car of its size. But off-road is where it excelled. It was so much smoother over the rough stuff than a leaf-sprung Land Rover, and yet had greater axle articulation and arguably better off-road ability. It also had a permanent four-wheel drive system, where the centre transfer box contained a differential feeding the front and rear propshafts – lesser off-roaders were rear-wheel drive until a leaver was thrown to engage the front prop, too, but without a centre diff they could never use 4WD on the road or else the props would wind up and compromise safe handling and durability – so the Range Rover was a revelation.

The Range Rover was redesigned – with a new grille and four doors – and the Vogue model was born. It's seen here lugging a heavy race car trailer up a gravel track.

Although the concept of a luxury estate car that could go anywhere was revolutionary in the UK, it had been about over the pond for seven years in the form of the 1963 Jeep Wagoneer. However, the Range Rover was launched with a remarkable lack of interior; just simple fabric seats, a minimalist dash, and rubber mats instead of carpets.

Immediately, engineering companies saw its potential; like a blank canvas ready for a masterpiece to be painted on. Overfinch stepped up to the challenge, and not only decked out the interior in luxury wood and leather but also offered the option of fitting a 5.7-litre Chevrolet V8.

Enthusiasts and engineering companies realised the chassis' huge potential in competition, and started putting Series Land Rover bodies on it. (Courtesy Drew Bowler)

At the same time, various enterprising enthusiasts had taken the coil-sprung chassis, trimmed the ends, and put it under Land Rover Series bodywork to make a superbly capable utility or competition vehicle. Whether the executives at Rover noticed this or not is unknown, but plans were put in place to do exactly that to the replacement for the Land Rover Series III. As an intermediate step a Series III chassis with the V8 and flat-fronted bodywork was put into limited production. Known as the Stage One, it heralded the look that the Defender would carry for three decades.

In 1983, the new Land Rover was

First called the Land Rover 90 and later Defender, the coil-sprung chassis brought the iconic Land Rover brand to a new generation.

launched. Known as a Land Rover 90 or 110, it had the coil-sprung chassis, axles, and powertrain from the Range Rover, but with a number of detail changes. The rear brakes were drums, a strange retrograde move done for political reasons rather than good engineering. Curiously, the 110 models had a higher capacity rear Salisbury differential even though the same torque was applied to both front and rear diffs, and it was never offered in the front as standard. The use of the Series Land

Doing what Land Rovers do; a standard Defender on a Green Lane trip easily tackles a river crossing.

Rover front bulkhead meant that the body was narrower than the axles, requiring wheelarch extensions to stay legal. For people needing the full width for large loads, a special pick up load bed was made, designated Hi Capacity.

The model range was renamed Defender in 1990 to distinguish it from the new Land Rover Discovery.

The defender was available on a 127in wheelbase by special order, and 6x6 variants sold in small quantities; often used as forestry and airport fire tenders.

The Range Rover was getting increasingly upmarket, and a gap was opening up for a more utilitarian car that still had the same level of refinement but allowed the new generation of adventure seekers to throw their mountain bikes in the back and strap their kayaks to the roof rack.

The club ethos is stronger today than ever before. Here, the Discovery Owners Club is supporting a race event at Pendine Sands, Wales.

And so the Discovery was born. The interior was designed with help from Terrance Conran and featured a light and airy space with many stowage areas and a passenger grab handle – presumably for moments of panic as the car negotiates mountainous tracks at extreme angles. The car featured a built-in roof rack with removable side slats, which stowed in a small bag under the rear seat to reduce drag – these were actually from a Maestro van.

The discovery arrived in 1989 and proved immensely popular with families, adventurers, and enthusiasts alike.

The rear seat was always positioned a little higher than the front seats on a Range Rover, which reduced headroom in the back. The Discovery solved this problem by increasing roof height just behind the B-pillar, and the extra space meant another set of occasional use seats could be fitted in the rear, turning it into a seven-seater. Cunningly, to make it look smaller than a Range Rover, the rear bodywork and load bed on the Discovery was a few inches shorter and the rear door was angled forwards.

The discovery received a substantial makeover in 1994, to coincide with the introduction of the 300Tdi diesel engine, and the design would continue until the Discovery 2 in 1999. Gone were the Sherpa headlights, and larger, more efficient units were installed. Some of the rear lights were moved to the bumper, and a better dash unit with superior dual-zone heater was installed.

The defender continued on, almost untouched by time as the company was passed from one owner to the next, but eventually the TD5 production line was nearing the end of its life, and so a suitable engine from the Ford range was sought. This coincided with a new Transit diesel engine going into production: code-named Puma, it was a thoroughly modern common rail diesel designed for the hard work a Transit van has to contend with. On paper it seemed ideal, apart from the fact that it didn't fit. Careful juggling of the engine and its six-speed gearbox resulted in a higher installation angle, necessitating a new bonnet design with distinctive bulge.

It's amazing that a chassis system first driven in the '60s was still in production over 40 years later. But the world has changed, and new crash regulations, pedestrian safety, and a host of other requirements are just too great a challenge for that classic design.

However, that will definitely not be the end of the story; the coil-sprung chassis capability and availability will keep us enthusiasts using and modifying these fantastic cars for a very long time yet.

Many investigations have been made into a Defender replacement. This experimental car is on display at the Heritage Museum, Gaydon.

Chapter 2
Racing

Could the chaps at Land Rover have had any idea back in the late '60s that their new creation would become a world beating race machine? Probably not.

The mixture of supple all-terrain suspension and a powerful V8 proved irresistible to the motorsport community, and it was not long before highly tuned Range Rovers were out competing in the toughest rallies in the world. And as the Defender and Discovery models were released, their own unique character would be exploited in a variety of race series, from rallies to winching challenges. The Camel Trophy famously used Land Rovers for its international adventure competitions; battling through forests, jungles, rock-strewn rivers and having to build improvised bridges along the way. This format was further developed by Land Rover itself in the G4 Challenge, which pushed the cars even more. Now there's a huge range of fantastic motorsport events across the whole world for all types of Land Rover,

Flying Land Rover: built by Bowler Off-road, taking a massive jump in its stride. (Courtesy Bowler)

and equally there are small club events held locally that are open to every enthusiast. There really is something for everyone. Here are just a few events to give a flavour of the remarkable range of possibilities.

Ready for takeoff: another Bowler streaks down the beach near the end of the Dakar Rally Raid. (Courtesy Bowler)

THE DAKAR RALLY RAID

Perhaps the greatest race in the world. Originally the Paris-Dakar Rally, it took competitors from France, through Spain, into Morocco, and down through the Sahara, before emerging on the west coast of Africa and into Dakar itself. On the way, drivers encountered deep mud, large rocks, rivers, and, of course, endless sand. This sort of event is many times more gruelling than a 'normal' rally, and so it has become known as a Rally Raid event. There are many similar Raids all over the world but the Dakar remains 'the daddy' of them all.

Over the years the route has changed to cope with complex politics, criminal gangs, terrorist threats, unmapped minefields, and wars. In recent years it has had to avoid Dakar completely because it was just too dangerous to venture near: cars have faced being attacked, ambushed, and led into traps by extremely violent thieves, as well as incidents of villagers putting obstacles in the path of racers to deliberately cause a crash – just for their own sick amusement.

But even when people are not conspiring against the cars, the terrain most definitely is. Sand gets rammed into every component, grinding away at critical parts in the suspension and drive line. It's treacherous stuff and can form rock hard ridges which punish car and driver as if racing over rocks, or it can be as soft as snow, which sucks the tyres into the ground and stops dead even the most powerful cars. There are huge temperature variations in the desert; below freezing at night and scorching highs during the day often, which often exceed 50°C.

This is why the race has become synonymous with the toughest vehicles and drivers in the world, and why global car companies spend many millions making special vehicles to take on the challenge; VW, Mitsubishi, and even Porsche, which competed a 4x4 911 (959) in the early days.

The Dakar has everything to challenge the toughest cars, including rock-strewn rivers and dense foliage. (Courtesy Bowler)

This is what the Dakar is famous for; sand and plenty of it. The race is usually over 5000 miles long, and each day might take in over 500 miles at very high speed. (Courtesy Bowler)

Land Rover entered the first Paris-Dakar race in 1979 with a works Range Rover, and won! This amazing testament to the high-performance, all-terrain capability of the coil-sprung chassis was repeated two years later, proving it was no fluke.

But privateer teams also enter the event, making up about 80 per cent of the field. It's remarkable just how many Land Rovers have been thrown at the challenge over the years. There's even a classic Jaguar XJ6 that, under the skin, has a space frame of steel tube supporting Range Rover axles, gearbox, and a race-tuned 4.2-litre Rover V8 – quite a sight.

In '87/'88 the Range Rover was given a thorough makeover in the form of the Holt-Up/Camel team. The chassis received a full tube space frame, the engine was moved back, and the bodywork was made of kevlar/carbon. These models were powered by JE-built 4.2-litre V8 engines that propelled them at up to 125mph on the rough, aided by aerodynamically tuned styling; with increased windscreen rake angle and a sloping bonnet, coupled with minimal overhangs. In '87 one car finished 2nd, and in '88 they finished 3rd and 4th. Considering that out of the 603 starters only 151 vehicles managed to finish the 8000 mile event at all, this was quite an achievement.

Most notable, however, are the Bowler cars, which superficially look like Defenders, and regularly inhabit the upper bands of the results tables, made on their own high strength space frame chassis with heavily uprated Land Rover mechanical parts.

Privateer-entered Range Rovers and Defenders have also competed in the Production classes, with little more than added safety equipment and race suspension, which is true testament to the strength of the original design.

Bowler's party trick: the sump guard hinges down to raise the car off the road for rapid wheel changes. This is the next generation Range Rover Sport-based Bowler Nemesis.

It might look like a Defender but its plastic body is built on a Range Rover rolling chassis, an ideal Comp Safari tool. (Courtesy Bowler)

Comp Safari classes cater for all types of car, such as this production-based Defender powering through a corner at speed. (Courtesy N Blundell)

Top Dakar mods

• Because of the extreme length of this race – individual stages can be over 500 miles in a day – the cars need to have a very long fuel range, and often three high capacity fuel tanks are fitted. The Discovery 2 derived Bowler Wildcat can carry up to 372 litres of fuel.

• On such a long race there's a strong possibility that tyres will get damaged, so cars often carry three spare wheels with a cunning method of changing them quickly. The Bowler Wildcats have a very clever system where the gearbox protection plate is hinged at the front and has a hydraulic ram at the back, so that, at the flick of a switch, it swings down and raises the whole car off the ground, making wheel changes very swift.

• The FIA rules require all cars on desert stages to carry at least ten litres of drinking water, an extensive emergency kit with first aid supplies, and the official radio communications system.

• Cars also have a built-in drinking system so the crew can take in liquid through a small drinking tube, usually built into their crash helmets.

• Damage is almost inevitable so the cars have to carry spares and an emergency tool kit, including a large roll of tank tape.

• Navigation is a matter of life and death so a full GPS racing trip computer is the co-driver's best friend.

• Running for such long distances flat out means the dampers are being bashed up and down relentlessly, making them very hot, so the damper oil is stored in remote reservoirs and cooling air is channelled over them. Some cars run double or triple dampers to share the load.

COMP SAFARI

Whilst the costs involved in a Rally Raid like the Dakar are prohibitive to most enthusiasts, a Competitive Safari is fairly affordable, but still has thrills and spills aplenty – much like a rally on steroids! There are fast gravel tracks through forests and fields where top speeds can be faster than World Rally Cars. Then there are river crossings with deep water and rocks that no rally car could ever attempt. There are sudden drops, cliff edges, steep rises, drainage ditches, deep mud, rocks, and jumps. The terrain is extreme and the cars have to be just as extreme to stand a chance of getting to the end, let alone winning.

In stark contrast to the hostile and aggressive nature of the course, the people involved are the friendliest and most helpful bunch you could ever wish to meet. Damage to cars is commonplace, but no sooner does a battered and wounded machine limp into the pits, everyone descends upon it to offer help, spare parts, advice, and usually a mug of tea.

A course is laid out over a distance of between 3 and 15 miles. The cars are let out one at a time and repeat the course up to ten times over the day, to make a total mileage of between 20 and 150 miles of high speed all-terrain action.

The machinery involved is divided into classes, so everyone can compete against similar cars to their own. There's a standard class for virtually unmodified vehicles; they need extra safety equipment such as a certified roll cage and harnesses to cope with the ever present danger of a major crash at high speed. This class is very popular with Defenders and stripped out Discoveries.

Moving up through the classes, the machinery gets more modified and more expensive. Many racers are based on the Land Rover coil-sprung chassis, but with a lightweight minimalist body grafted on. Favourites include vehicles from 3M, QT, and Tomcat (covered in more detail in chapter 9), which can weigh in at less than 1300kg, and when coupled with race-tuned V8s or diesels, make for extremely fast and capable packages at a fraction of the cost of a World Rally Car.

Some cars, such as the Simbugini, use Land Rover axles, engine, and gearbox on a custom tube frame; nothing of the original chassis exists and the whole car is much lower than standard. The engine is mounted backwards in the rear of the car and the diffs are inverted in the axles to

Some specials use only the engine and gearbox from Land Rover, combined with a full space frame chassis and bespoke independent suspension.
(Courtesy N Blundell)

An early Bowler Tomcat in minimalist form; chassis, seats, and a cage. What more do you need?
(Courtesy Bowler)

A more advanced Tomcat with 'hockey stick' rear suspension, and a full body to make dealing with water at high speed more pleasant. (Courtesy Bowler)

compensate. These machines are astonishingly fast off-road and speeds well in excess of 120mph are common on long straights.

Keeping weight down is vital, so there are no bull bars or winches here, recovery equipment is limited to sturdy towing points and a tow rope. The general theory is that if you get stuck you weren't going fast enough!

This is a spectacular sport and amazingly accessible for ordinary folk. It's definitely worth visiting an event and you are sure to get some fantastic pictures.

Top Comp Safari mods
• Remove all unnecessary weight; if it's not needed, cut it off.

• Roll cage is mandatory: attached securely to the chassis.
• Underbody protection: skid plate under the engine and gearbox, plus diff guards.
• Really good windscreen wipers, sometimes triple arms, and using headlight washer jets to blast mud off the screen.
• Race seats and harnesses – getting thrown around violently means that the occupants have to be held in very securely.
• Fire extinguisher – a handheld unit is mandatory, but plumbed-in systems that flood the engine bay with powder are favoured on the top machines.
• Snorkel and waterproofing – there are often river crossings, and hitting even a big puddle at speed forces water everywhere.
• Bobbin engine mounts stop the engine ripping away when big jumps are taken at speed.
• Radiator mounted in the back to prevent damage and blockage from mud.

CHALLENGE
Challenge events pit the driver and navigator against the toughest natural obstacles the world has to offer, and some not so natural obstacles, too. Sometimes the path is un-driveable and the winch is the only way to continue – the navigator has to leap out, grab the recovery equipment, run to the other side of the obstacle and then secure anchor points and get the winch rope attached – so fitness is as important as skill.

The idea is to reach one or more

Challenge events involve getting the car into places only reachable with a strong winch. The co-driver has to be very fit ... (Courtesy Devon 4x4)

... and waterproof! Treacherous terrain ahead means the winch needs to be employed as the car drives across this swamp. (Courtesy Devon 4x4)

Building a race car is about attention to detail; reliability and durability are as essential as power and performance. (Courtesy Devon 4x4)

The Devon 4x4 Challenge truck before it gets dirty: a machine built for a single purpose with highly accessible recovery kit, high suspension, full cage, and winches. (Courtesy Devon 4x4)

inaccessible points shown on a map and recover proof that the car has been there, usually from a stamp that is attached to the target location.

But time is also a factor so the car has to be as fast as possible from point to point; power and manoeuvrability are vital as the car tackles boulders, rivers, mud pits, undercut cliffs and sand. Every event offers something different in the terrain and, as well as the big obstacles, there are usually high speed sprints on rough tracks linking them all together. In many ways this is the purest form of off-road competition as it includes something from every other discipline; high speed, low speed, and recovery.

The cars have to be very rugged as well as manoeuvrable. The Defender 90 is a very popular choice, and modifications transform it utterly. All overhang is removed – some of the obstacles are cliffs that are like driving up a brick wall, so any overhang would foul. Usually, the body behind the cab is completely removed and replaced with a tray that has recovery gear, such as waffle boards and ground anchors, easily available. Often, two winches are fitted. The one at the front does most of the work, but a rear-mounted winch is invaluable when the only way out is back the way you went in. To pull the front winch rope out quickly when needed it's often laid out in a zigzag across the bonnet, and held in place with an elasticated net. The navigator can then simply grab the hook and run as the rope pulls free.

Top Challenge mods

• Winches, high power, and fast motors are needed as time is critical. Some vehicles have a central-mounted winch that runs the rope through a fairlead on the top of the main roll hoop. This allows the car to winch itself upright if it rolls,

or prevents a roll when tackling extreme side slopes.
- Tray-back to reduce weight and provide instant access to recovery gear.
- No overhangs or bumpers.
- Full external roll cage.
- Race trip computer and GPS system.
- Recovery equipment including waffle boards, shackles, tree strops, and ground anchors.
- Spare wheel and high lift jack for rapid changes.
- Full underbody protection and jackable sills.
- Long- and short-range spotlights on a foldable frame.
- Dislocating rear suspension and relocation cones.
- Extreme long-travel suspension with highly articulated damper and axle mounts.
- Extreme angle propshafts.
- Snorkel and wading kit.
- Large diameter tyres with very large tread lugs, bead lock, or bead protector.

TRIALLING

Not all racing is about speed. Trialling is all about getting as far as possible along a very difficult path. A course is set out that usually involves very tight turns, twists, and always a very steep slope, and gets progressively more difficult until the last part is nigh on impossible. The course is divided into sections, usually ten, and marked out with poles and tape. The car scores points according to how far up the course it gets before getting stuck or rolling backwards. If it drives outside the marked course it has failed that section.

The beauty of this form of sport is that competitive cars can be made very cheaply; power isn't important and super-strength components are not needed.

There isn't one perfect solution: a short wheelbase makes tight turns

Trialling is all about low speed car control and good visibility, which is achieved here by removing unwanted bodywork. The side slope tipped the car perilously close to the marker pole. (Courtesy Bowler)

Trialling has classes for completely standard road cars like this Discovery, making it the most accessible form of motorsport.

easier but a longer wheelbase is better on steep hills, so the mix of machinery makes for interesting results. There's ample scope for innovation and trying out ideas without breaking the bank; in fact, it's very easy to get obsessively involved in thinking through technicalities and pondering tyre pressures.

Tyre pressures are the most crucial tuning method available. Generally, they're set very low, although often the regulations have a lower limit. A good

starting point is 15psi, which allows the tyre to flex and grab hold of the terrain, as well as spread the load over a wider area.

There are many situations where the car will be inclined at a steep angle and in danger of rolling over, so an external roll cage is a really good idea. It can also provide lashing points for recovery if the car does roll-over.

The range of cars competing can vary immensely. At one extreme are cars with almost everything removed –

This machine used for Challenge and Trials events sports a few battle scars. Note the wing (fender) is actually a steel tube frame with ally (aluminium) panels riveted on – very clever.

only a bulkhead and floor for bodywork and all overhang cut off. At the other extreme are absolutely standard road cars with only safety equipment added. Course severity varies, too, depending on the class of cars competing. There really is something for everyone and it's one of the easiest ways to take part in motorsport.

A typical day will have ten different courses laid out and often the course will be driven twice, once in each direction. Most people walk the course first, deciding which is the best line and how much momentum will need to be carried through each section. It becomes easy to get engrossed in analysing the ground, particularly after the first few runs have been completed and experience develops.

Trialling is hugely engaging and wonderfully accessible. Gaining new driving skills can be very rewarding, too. No wonder many racers get hooked and continue competing well into their retirement years.

Top Trialling mods
- Quality tyres run at low pressure.
- Remove any unnecessary weight.
- Minimal roll cage.
- Electric fan.

GETTING INVOLVED

Motorsport is usually expensive and competing isn't for everyone, but there are still ways to get involved. All motorsports rely on an army of volunteers such as marshals, who wave flags to warn racers of hidden dangers, report incidents to race control, and are first on scene if there's an accident. Not only are marshals the first line in emergency response but they're the eyes, ears, and arms of the race controllers – without them there wouldn't be any races.

Being a marshal has many advantages: firstly, you get to see loads of racing close up for free; secondly, being part of the sport is very rewarding, and if you are thinking of taking part one day it gives a very useful insight into the best and worst techniques. Also, the training and responsibility looks good on a CV as it shows reliability and a willingness to take part.

Marshals are always in short supply and even if you are only able to spare a few days a year your participation will be greatly appreciated.

WHAT MAKES A RACING CAR?

You might think that race cars are all about tuning the engine and suspension, but very often the engine is kept as standard as possible to keep it reliable. There's an old phrase in racing 'to finish first, first you have to finish' and the greatest part of the engineering effort is put into making the car reliable and durable. For high speed events things like bobbin engine mounts, which can't rip apart, and reinforced suspension mounting points are crucial, as is stopping the radiator being damaged or clogged and fitting double throttle return springs in case one breaks. Keeping the screen clear is essential if the driver is to position the car accurately, so good demisters, and even having removable doors, can improve the view and make a car faster in the race.

Sometimes the performance figures for a competition car can seem uninspiring, but if a standard car with similar figures was to attempt the same Comp Safari or Rally Raid race the difference would soon become clear: the standard car would struggle to stay on the racing line and would constantly lose time compared to the competition prepared car. Eventually it would suffer damage that would force it to stop.

Race cars are amazing machines. At the top level there's ingenious engineering in every single component, most of the beauty is hidden from view but the fact that the car finishes the event shows that it works.

Chapter 3
Expeditions

A Camel train? Over 1000 miles of hard work will test these Discoveries to the absolute limit. (Courtesy Land Rover PR)

These cars make superb expedition vehicles; not only can they tackle the worst roads in the world but they have excellent interior space and load capacity for carrying supplies and spares. Unlike leaf-sprung competitors, the coil-sprung chassis smooths the roughest road, which reduces driver fatigue and gives the car body an easier life, too. This fact was noticed by explorers right from the start, and it wasn't long before Range Rovers were fitted with roof racks and reinforced bumpers prior to travelling to the remotest parts of the globe.

Expeditions don't always have to be extreme, they can be anything you want; from a week's camping trip right up to a round the world tour. Whatever you want to do and wherever you want to go, exploring in your Land Rover can be a very rewarding experience – just remember to take your camera!

CAMEL TROPHY/G4

The Camel Trophy is legendary in Land Rover circles, but it originally started in 1980 with three German teams using Jeeps. This was supposed to be a one-off but the publicity was so great that Camel instigated a regular yearly expedition, which visited some of the wildest and most treacherous places on the planet. From 1981 to 1998, the event was sponsored by Land Rover, initially with Range Rovers but later using Discoveries and Defenders, too – all vehicles were heavily modified for safety and reliability in the tough conditions.

The events were intended to test the competitors' endurance, ingenuity, stamina, skill, and teamwork as they faced routes that were barely passable on foot let alone in a car. Bridges had to be made, paths cut into dense jungle, and deep rocky bedded rivers forded, often with water up to roof height. Most of the events had environmental goals, too – one event saw competitors build

Land Rover returned to the great expedition with the G4 Challenge; much the same formula but now in orange. (Courtesy Land Rover PR)

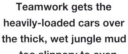

Teamwork gets the heavily-loaded cars over the thick, wet jungle mud – too slippery to even stand on. (Courtesy Land Rover PR)

This is why the cars have snorkels, and lights in the roof rack. The mirror was 'shaved' off in an earlier incident. (Courtesy Land Rover PR)

an environmental monitoring station in the middle of the jungle. Generally, routes consisted of abandoned and destroyed old tracks, and the teams reopened them as they went, benefiting the local population to some extent.

The cars were worked to their absolute limits, as were the competitors, but breakdowns were very rare, despite many cars being rolled. Every car wore the distinctive 'Sandglow' yellow paint (actually an old BL colour: STC1489/A) and Camel logos, but as time went by Land Rover came under increasing pressure to disassociate from any possible link with tobacco. Various public excuses were made about the event no longer being in the 'spirit of Land Rover' and its support was withdrawn in 1999. The 2000 event was run using boats instead, and proved very successful, but a company buyout saw the Camel brand concentrate on clothing rather than international adventures.

This left a huge void for enthusiasts who had come to love the event, and pressure mounted on Land Rover to instigate something similar. In 2003 the Land Rover G4 'ultimate global adventure' series was born, with a format like the 1998 Camel event. Defenders were the last of the old coil-sprung cars to compete; all cars were painted 'Tangiers Orange' and had similar modifications to the Camel cars.

Top Camel Trophy/G4 mods

- Substantial full roll cage from Safety Devices.
- Underbody protection plates and steering guard.
- Front bumper-mounted winch.
- Dixon Bate tow hitch and tow points.
- Bull bars with brush wires.
- Brownchurch roof rack.
- Auxiliary long-range fuel tanks.
- Mantec snorkel.
- Extended transmission and axle breathers.
- Heavy-duty suspension and transmission parts.
- Michelin XCL or BFG MT tyres.
- Websto fuel burning heaters.

• Extra Hella driving, spot, fog convoy, and work lights.
• Electrical system modified for extra circuits and waterproofing.
• Expedition tools, spares, fuel and water cans.
• Extensive navigation and trip computer equipment.

DARIEN GAP

The Darien Gap is a stretch of land between Central and North America, it remains the only part of America that doesn't have a road. The Pan American Highway stretches 29,800 miles from Chile to Alaska, except this 99-mile gap. The reason it has defeated all attempts to make a drivable path is that the terrain ranges from thick rain forest on mountainous rock at altitudes of up to 6000ft, down to deep swamp land that stretches for miles. So it's a bit tricky!

Faced with any impossible path it's only human nature to try and complete it, and the Darien Gap is no different. The first vehicular crossing was made in 1960 by a Series Land Rover and a Jeep. It took 136 days, averaging about 0.2mph.

In 1972, the splendidly-named British Trans-Americas Expedition, lead by the equally splendidly-named John Blashford-Snell, took two Range Rovers along the whole Pan American Highway, including the Gap.

To be fair, he did have backup from a large part of the British Army: the Royal Engineers went ahead cutting trees and building bridges, aided by a team of 30 horses, supplies were airlifted in by the Army Air Corps, and for most of the route the cars were driven by men from the 17th/21st Lancers. Also, the expedition missed out the worst part of the huge Atrato swamp and river in Colombia by taking a short boat trip, but even so it was a remarkable achievement for near standard cars with no strengthening at all – the adventure was chronicled in the book *The Hundred Days of Darien* written in 1974. Tackling the rocks and dense jungle required underbody protection and substantial bumpers. Extra storage provisions and a strong roof rack allowed all the necessary equipment to be taken, which is essential when you are a few months' drive away from the nearest shop.

Carrying all the heavy equipment and using oversize tyres put excessive strain on the standard differentials, which wore out. After replacements from Rover were flown in, and normal size tyres were fitted, the expedition continued without further breakdown.

Now that's a serious adventure!

Top Darien Gap mods

• Two spare wheels mounted to the front of the roof.
• Substantial roof rack.
• Double bumper made from two Range Rover bumpers, one mounted above the other and joined by steel bars.
• Wing mirrors.
• Fuel tank guard.
• Heavy-duty towing eyes.
• Engine snorkel.
• Engine-driven Fairey capstan winch.
• Auxiliary halogen spot lamps and windscreen pillar-mounted swivel lights.
• Twin battery split charge system.
• 12x16.5in or 7.50x16 Firestone Super All-Traction swamp tyres .
• Removable wing panels for easier wheel access.
• Roll-over bar.

The two Darien Gap Range Rovers with bridging ladders on their roofs. An astonishing expedition for near standard cars. (Courtesy Land Rover PR)

- Cold climate dampers, hydraulic hoses and clutch plate.
- Heated rear screen with washer and wiper (at that time not fitted on standard cars).
- Extra dash gauges, including rev counter, oil pressure and temperature.
- Two-way radio.
- Single reclining rear seat.
- A pair of lightweight aluminium bridging ladders.
- One of the cars had a built-in safe for passports and money.

THE ROAD TO KATHMANDU

Expeditions don't have to be arduous trials on punishing terrain, they can be travelling on established tracks to destinations new to you (maybe Kathmandu or Morocco), but well-known to many other adventurers and travellers who regularly run these routes. It can be a great opportunity to take in stunning scenery and experience other cultures. The trip can be totally focused on the journey and surroundings, with the car as just a tool to get you there.

Many clubs offer well organised expeditions for between one and ten week durations; one and two week trips

Many roads around the world are rough gravel or dirt, easily washed away in places, but the Land Rover keeps on going, despite this.

On club expeditions there's plenty of time to stop and admire the scenery.

are very popular as they can fit in with work commitments. Often, expeditions are inspired by some great historical theme, following an ancient trade route or recreating the path of a great explorer, with stop-overs in magnificent locations and passing through spectacular scenery.

Travelling in another country provides new types of terrain but, unlike local off-road trips, the idea isn't to tackle huge obstacles because getting stuck thousands of miles from home is usually a

very bad thing. The challenge of an expedition is in the scale of the journey and personal achievement. Of course, it may not always be just driving down a nice road, sometimes in far flung places difficult routes have to be taken; bridges can be out, roads can be washed away, and landslides might obstruct the track. These obstacles can test the best off-road skills and sometimes it's better to turn round and try a different route. Ability to accurately assess the terrain is as vital as vehicle preparation.

If you fancy a really big challenge there are regular organised major expeditions that cross continents, sampling the fascinating trails that each country has to offer.

Crossing Africa has many peculiarities, including avoiding war zones, bandits, and uncharted minefields. Giant deserts pose the twin challenges of sand and navigation. Dunes can be rock hard on the down-wind side and soft as powder snow on the up-wind side, and often flat sand can form hard ripples which test the cars' suspension as if driving over cobble stones. It's very easy to get lost in a desert, the dunes are constantly moving and reshaping, and often there are no distinct features for a great many miles. Navigation equipment is essential, and sometimes so is a local guide.

Tackling a long expedition in a coil-sprung model requires good preparation due to its age. Ensure the chassis and mechanical parts are in good order before starting. Although, if it's all OK, a Land Rover is ideal for taking on the worst roads the world can

Expeditions don't have to be death-defying jungle treks. Travelling to remote and spectacular places on roads and tracks is still a fantastic adventure.

Travelling with like-minded friends and companions adds to the fun, and means there's help if you get stuck.

throw at it – after all that is what they were made for!

Top Travellers' mods

- Spare parts tucked away securely.
- Durable tyres: some journeys favour commercial van tyres which are much longer-lasting.
- Extra storage for luggage and fluids: roof rack and external jerry can holders for water.
- A full service is essential before starting.
- Navigation equipment.
- A hand winch for self-recovery.
- First aid kit.
- Auxiliary fuel tanks.
- Underbody protection.

SPARES

Most of these cars need a service every 5000 miles, so long expeditions need to take enough oil, filters, grease, and replacement parts for the duration, or alternatively book ahead with trusted service stations on the way. Either way there's still the potential for the unexpected, so it's worth taking a few useful spares in case of problems when the car is miles from help. It's also sensible to research the service stations on the route – find out from other

travellers which ones should be avoided and which are super helpful. Spare parts need to be added to the Carnet de Passage to avoid having to pay import tax at every border crossing.

The most common breakages are: dampers due to rough roads; brake pads due to grit and water abrasion; engine mounts due to pot holes; the radiator due to stones being thrown up by traffic; plus lights damaged in minor accidents. The screen will be tested on gravel roads, with the vibration turning chips into cracks very easily, so a windscreen chip repair kit is very useful. If the screen does get broken then a roll of clear sticky-back plastic can effect a temporary repair.

The most important things in the spares kit will always be tie-wraps and tank (duct) tape. Armed with these, a broken body panel, dislodged light cluster, or a myriad of loose components can be fixed back in place until a permanent repair can be made. These should be considered essentials.

TYRES – THE KEY TO SURVIVAL

The first consideration is the tyres. Not only do they need to be suitable for the terrain but also very durable. On

long expeditions it's quite common to carry two spare wheels and a further two tyres not on wheels. Another vital consideration when choosing tyres is fuel economy. Big wobbly tread blocks waste power and this means more frequent fuel stops. On some trips this can be a matter of life and death. Trans-Sahara Land Rovers frequently have massive auxiliary fuel tanks, sometimes several hundred litres. It's a good idea to fit two big tanks and refuel only one tank at each stop in countries where fuel quality can be poor; after refuelling, the fresh tank is used for the first few miles, and if the fuel turns out to be suspect then the other tank can be used and the plan changed to fit in an extra stop.

The most important component isn't the car.

This book is about modifying cars, but successful expeditions also need a huge amount of research to understand the terrain, legalities, stopping points, and, crucially, refuelling points. The best starting point is to have a chat with someone who has done it already – getting the right advice not only makes an expedition go a lot smoother but in some cases it can save your life.

Long expeditions need the driver to be just as prepared as the car. Fitness is very important if you are going to be driving for long periods because it aids concentration and alertness. If travelling in extreme cold or hot climates fitness is even more important, and staying in good shape will make maintenance and repairs easier and safer, too.

When researching the trip it's vital to check the type of terrain that you will encounter on every stage of the journey. This information is essential when working out how to prepare the vehicle.

Luckily, there are loads of fellow enthusiasts who will be very happy to tell you all about it.

Chapter 4
Trekking

So, having seen what the car is capable of in extreme situations, what is available for ordinary enthusiasts? Well, it turns out that there's quite a large range of fun activities, most of which don't need any special skills or vehicle modifications.

The first option is to explore the countryside on road that the Land Rover was built for, a gentle but rewarding experience that the whole family can join in.

Driving tracks and Green Lanes can transport you to wonderful and remote parts of the country.

The second is to have fun at one of the 'Pay and Play' events. These are often held in disused quarries or muddy valleys, and allow the driver to explore the full off-road capabilities in relatively safe surroundings. Everyone I have ever seen take part in these events comes away with a very big smile, so go on and have some fun.

GREEN LANES

Green Laning is a pastime enjoyed by hundreds of off-road enthusiasts every weekend in the UK. Green Lanes are simply public roads that don't have a hard surface; no tarmac or concrete in sight. Most are a mixture of gravel, stone, and dirt, and some have small river crossings. It's a fantastic way to get away from the rat run of the city, and enjoy the countryside on routes that offer interesting driving terrain and spectacular scenery. The roads are tackled slowly and with caution. The idea is to spend all day exploring and

On long trips the weather can turn nasty, and very quickly roads can become rivers.

enjoying the country. It's definitely *not* a high speed mud bath Play Day, but driven appropriately these tracks are very rewarding and lots of fun.

Land Rover promotes the TREAD lightly policy which is a mnemonic for:
Travel only where permitted: double check you are allowed on a route.
Respect the rights of others: roads are for everyone; be courteous and leave tracks in good condition.
Educate yourself about the route: some go through farm land and gates must be

closed. Know what obstacles are ahead and drive accordingly.

Avoid sensitive areas: don't cut up soft ground and do preserve wild habitats. Drive responsibly: 4x4s get a bad press, so when out and about every one of us should be an ambassador for the activity.

Sometimes rivers can be quite deep. Checking ahead is vital to avoid submerged pot holes. (Courtesy Land Rover PR)

It's vital to fully research the route beforehand, and local knowledge is very helpful. The best source is from local off-road clubs, and from the Green Lane Association (GLASS), which I strongly recommend joining if you are in the UK – similar organisations exist in most countries.

They will be able to guide you onto the most suitable and rewarding routes, taking into account your experience and vehicle type.

The car must be fully road legal, so in the UK that requires tax, insurance, and MoT because these are public roads. These roads are just the same as those in the High Street, shared by walkers, horses, bikes, and motorcycles, so normal road rules apply.

All routes need to be cared for. Driving aggressively will erode the surface and ruin it for other users. Also, if you go too fast and have an accident miles from any help you are in lots of trouble. And a word of caution: it's very

easy to have an accident by going just one or two mph faster than necessary, so if it's your first time go with an old hand who will show you how to look after yourself and the road.

Many off-road clubs take this duty of care very seriously and spend a few days every year maintaining lanes and repairing natural erosion. This is a wonderful way to get involved with both the club and the countryside, well worth volunteering for.

Going through farm land, it's essential to leave the gates as you found them.

Totally standard Land Rovers are ideal for this terrain – it's what they were built for.

Top Green Lane mods

• Any of the Land Rovers covered in this book should be able to head out on a Green Lane without any modification – that's what makes Land Rovers so great – but there are a few modifications that can make the day easier and more pleasant.

• As ever, tyres are the key to success. Aggressive treads should be avoided as they can damage some sections

of the track. Any good quality road or all-terrain tyre with reasonable tread depth should do the job very well. One of the trickiest surfaces is wet grass on a hill – low tread depth will make this an impossible obstacle.

• Fitting brush wires can help with small overhanging branches, but there shouldn't be anything worse than that in the way so bull bars are not really needed.

• Generally, progress is slow, so make sure the cooling system is working well. The standard visco drive fan is great when it's working properly, but replacing it with an electric fan and an interior switch allows it to be switched off when wading through deep water. The engine driven fan can be excessively loaded in water.

• Before wading ensure the wading plugs are in the bell housing, depending on model. Early cars had low mounted axle and transmission breathers, which should be extended up higher (usually fixed to the top of the bulkhead) as some crossings can result in water up to the top of the tyres.

• These trips can last a day or longer, so reliability is essential. Ensure the car is fully serviced beforehand, checking the hub seals in particular as these will let water in and eventually cause bearing failure if old or worn.

• It's worth fitting extra storage bins for maps and food. There's always a possibility of getting stuck and having to wait for rescue so warm clothes, blankets, and supplies are a good idea. Often the trails will be a long way from help, so first aid kits and fire extinguishers should be taken.

• Usually several cars will go as a team, but it's recommended to limit this to about five. Choosing the right route should ensure you never get stuck, but there's always a risk so recovery equipment is essential. If you are going out alone (which isn't recommended) then a self-recovery winch can save the day. Bear in mind you will probably need to be recovered backwards, away from the danger area, and then proceed on a different route.

• Communication between vehicles is usually done with PMR or CB radio equipment. It's worth noting that often these areas will have no mobile phone coverage.

• When planning long trips into the countryside, fuel range can be a problem and travelling at low speeds on rough ground uses significantly more fuel than normal road use, so either plan fuel stops or carry extra capacity. Auxiliary fuel tanks are available for most variants, and, although generally best avoided for safety reasons, any fuel cans must be stowed securely and be leak free.

PAY AND PLAY DAYS

This is almost the complete opposite of Green Laning. There's much more freedom to muck about, get stuck, and test both your own and your car's abilities.

Most sites offer a wide range of terrains including deep mud, steep slopes, ruts, and banks. There are usually a set of well defined routes that are graded from very easy (ideal for the

Driving on private sites dedicated to off-road motoring provides much more challenging terrain.
(Courtesy Land Rover PR)

Pushing the car close to its limits can be fun and rewarding, but advice is essential for the novice. (Courtesy Land Rover PR)

Attaching the tow rope when the car has sunk in mud is no fun; this car already has the rope attached ready for the inevitable.

first timer), right up to impossible but fun to try.

Be warned though, this activity is very addictive and it's easy to push your vehicle beyond both its and your own abilities, and damage is commonplace as a result. If you drive within the limits then you will both be fine. Indeed, many people use these sites to develop their skills and also their car, so its capability grows at the same time. This can be a very rewarding way to enjoy your car, but as ever limits need to be applied to budgets and time so that it doesn't take over your life.

Because of likely damage, many people opt for having a dedicated Play Day car, trailering it to the event. This allows for much greater levels of modification than is possible on a car which also has to be road legal.

All in all, it's whatever you want to make of it; either a gentle bit of fun or a challenge for your skills and abilities. Either way, its lots of fun and generates the biggest grins possible.

Top Pay and Play mods

• Aggressive tyres are perfectly suited here, chunky mud terrains are usually best.

• Ground clearance is very valuable, so raised suspension and removal of overhangs, bobtail Range Rovers are popular.

• Cars can get very stuck, so good quality recovery points are important.

• With all those lumps and bumps some people go for more supportive seats, even racing style bucket seats and harnesses get fitted to some of the more extreme vehicles.

• Underbody protection is also a popular modification, particularly protection of the steering rods and the vulnerable front diff pan.

• Exhausts tend to get a battering and tail pipes can be easily squashed, so side exit exhausts are a handy modification.

• The more adventurous tracks present the spectre of rolling the car if taken too fast. Driven sensibly they're fine, but as a precaution some people fit roll cages. Although it should be remembered that fitting weighty items to the body actually makes it slightly more likely to roll.

A proud Land Rover owner (the author) after a hard day's playing in the mud.

Chapter 5
Buyers' guide

So, which one will you choose? Whether you are buying a car to have fun in the mud or to work hard lugging big loads, the older Land Rover range has huge potential, and with prices very low many people can now afford to build their dream project.

There are a huge number of variations to choose from; often there were several model changes per year, with varying levels of usefulness. Each has its own charm, but they all share the same DNA and can be extremely capable on or off-road, or even converted into an all-out racing car.

This chapter begins by describing each of the three models' evolution, and then, because most buying advice is applicable across the model range (check the sills, rear crossmember, etc), it explains the common aspects and things to check when looking at a car to buy.

RANGE ROVER

The RRC has been through a number of changes in its lifetime. Before its launch, a handful of preproduction cars were sold off, named Velar, but the main production run started in 1970 with the two-door model. Legend has it that the trim design was not ready in time, but whatever the real reason, the original interior was very sparse; no carpets, minimal dash, and simple vinyl

The original Classic Range Rover when launched in 1970 had a beautiful simplicity. (Courtesy Land Rover PR)

The original Classic Range Rover interior; simple but functional, and reasonably comfy. (Courtesy Land Rover PR)

seats. Although basic, it was still very comfortable and light and airy. All Land Rovers feature a 'wash out' interior: the sills are mounted under the floorpanel so the interior can be simply washed out without risk of mud puddling on the floorpan. However, it's better to think of it as a 'brush out' interior because the wiring and metalwork don't like water inside.

The Classic had a wheelbase of 100in and was fitted with a twin carburettor Rover V8 engine and four-speed LT95 gearbox, which had an integral transfer box. In most markets it was tuned to 135bhp and, with a kerb weight of just over 1700kg, performance was quite good for the time. This model had an open differential that split the torque equally between the front and rear axles, but if one started to spin on slippery ground a lever could be pulled to lock the centre differential. It was this permanent four-wheel drive system that was so revolutionary on a relatively luxurious road car at the time.

In 1973, power steering became a much needed option, but, other than a steady stream of minor mechanical changes, nothing much happened until 1980 when the suspension was lowered by 20mm to combat the high degree of body roll.

A few innovative engineering firms offered four-door conversions during this time, but the factory only produced two-door models until 1981 when its own four-door model was finally launched. In the UK, four-door demand outstripped two-door by 90 per cent and the two-door model was dropped 1985, remaining in production only for export markets such as France, where it was still very popular.

A two-door model was offered in basic 'Fleetline' configuration, with power steering only as an option, and a very basic interior. This was used by

Police forces and commercial users as a very capable, go anywhere workhorse.

An automatic transmission using the Chrysler Torqueflite A727 was introduced in 1982. This made for relaxing driving and was a taste of things to come, although with only three gears performance was not fantastic.

There was an increasing need for a diesel engine in the range, and in 1983 the Italian 2.4-litre VM diesel was introduced after work on the ill-fated 'Project Iceberg' – a diesel version of the Rover V8 – had finally ground to a halt. Performance was adequate but not inspiring, and if driven hard its reliability suffered.

These early models were offered with the full length Webasto retracting cloth sunroof, which can leak and corrode so check all the metalwork when fully retracted. The roof frame was modified and the rail above the windscreen was a different design to the standard roof unit, so swapping over requires a few modifications.

In 1983, a special run of 1000 'In Vogue' models were produced in association with the well-known fashion magazine. They were all painted 'Caspian Blue' and the interior was produced in association with Wood & Picket coach builders in London.

This, in turn, spawned the main production run of 'Vogue' models in 1985, distinguished by a change from a metal front grille with vertical slats to a plastic grille incorporating headlight trims with horizontal slats. It also saw the introduction of an under bumper spoiler incorporating fog lights, which,

The Range Rover underwent many changes. The Vogue model has the horizontal slatted grille, as well as some subtle modifications.

The later Vogue-style interior with plusher seats and revised dash.

unfortunately, is so low that it can easily be broken when off-road – even the Land Rover handbook recommends its removal before venturing into the rough stuff.

In the UK, the standard model was now the Vogue but most cars did not have any badging to say so. The only evidence was on the registration documents but even this was sporadic. The top-of-the-range model became the Vogue SE, which had all the toys, such as cruise control, leather seats, and air-conditioning.

There were a host of detail engineering updates at that time, too. The rear axle originally had one damper facing forwards and the other facing backwards, the Vogue had them both facing forwards. The auto gearbox option changed to the superior ZF 4HP22, and the manual option became the Rover LT77 five-speed from the SD1. Both these gearboxes used the new LT230 transfer box, a separate bolt-on item. The engine gained fuel-injection and more power, producing 165bhp using the Efi system and intake from the Rover SD1 Vitesse, but with a milder cam and lower compression to allow for a greater tolerance of poor fuels. However, many export markets retained carbs for many years to come.

The front 'hockey stick' radius arms became thicker and stronger when the axles became largely metric at some point in the early eighties.

The Range Rover was officially first imported into North America in 1986, and the project was code-named 'Eagle.' A number of detail changes were made so that the car would be more appealing to this market. Firstly, the generous panel gaps were thought too large and so production tolerances were reduced. This was partly achieved by reducing the number of bolted together parts on the steel frame, such as the radiator crossmember, and replacing them with welded versions instead.

From 1986, the transfer box changed to a Borg Warner unit that had a viscous limited slip differential. This illuminated the need for a diff lock function because only a very small amount of slip was allowed, just enough to allow for cornering.

The fuel filler cap finally got a flush fitting cover flap in 1987, initially with a key lock but later models had electronic locking.

That same year, the roof structure was revised so water channels would not obstruct the forthcoming sunroof

option of 1988. Also, the calibration of the auto gearbox was improved; torque converter lock up moved from 40mph to 50mph and the second gear ratio was changed to improve fuel economy.

In 1989, the V8 engine was produced with a wider bore to displace 3.9 litres, and the radiator supported an additional engine oil cooler that supplemented the standard one mounted in front of the radiator. Auto models also had a gearbox oil cooler in the radiator to help the 'bog brush'-type cooler mounted on the front crossmember. The interior was revised, and the axles gained a set of anti-roll bars (25mm front/18.5mm rear) to combat the extra roll caused by the increased weight from all the options available. The same year, the VM diesel engine grew to 2.5 litres.

The last small batch of 200 two-door bodyshells were uncovered in 1990 and put into production with the 3.9-litre V, a special trim level, and named CSK after one of the car's original creators, Charles Spencer King.

1990 also brought ABS from Wabco. It's a tricky thing making ABS work on a car that might have to drive down muddy banks and snow, which is why it took so long to come out. But the system works very well, although wheel sensors can take a bit of a battering and are the most likely failure point. This year also saw the introduction of vented

front brake disks. The new braking system reduced overall braking distance and helped maintain control in an emergency. The speedo changed from cable driven to electronic that year, too.

In 1991, the fuel tank and filler system changed. Earlier tanks were difficult to fill due to the filler being so low down, so the filler point was moved up onto the top of the rear wing, and the plastic fuel tank enlarged to occupy some of the space vacated by the old filler point.

The long wheelbase (108in) LSE arrived in 1992 with a long stroke

Air suspension in action; the car should glide to maximum and minimum height smoothly and evenly.

The last Range Rovers got a 'soft' dash based on the revised 300-style Discovery item.

4.2-litre V8 and air suspension, which replaced the coil springs with rubber air-bags, and allowed the ride height to be changed at the push of a button, although early systems proved unreliable. The North American market LSE models were the standard 100in 3.9-litre V8 cars until the LSE County was released.

The same year, the VM diesel was replaced with Rover's own 200Tdi unit, which was more powerful and efficient.

The final chapter started in 1994, when the Range Rover's replacement, code-named P38a, was launched. The original Range Rover carried on in production until 1996, under the name Range Rover Classic – a name that would stick and become synonymous with the whole first generation of the Range Rover. The '94 model was extensively upgraded, most noticeably with a Discovery derived 'Soft Dash' with twin air-bags. This model year also saw the replacement of the 200Tdi with the improved 300Tdi diesel engine.

DISCOVERY

Launched in 1989, the Discovery was designed with real purpose in mind. The interior was brilliantly appointed by Conran Design, and the exterior styling was designed to make it look smaller than its big brother, the Range

The next new model was the Discovery, launched in 1989 and targeted squarely at the leisure and family market.

The 200-style Discoveries had many parts from other BL models, such as these Sherpa headlights, and Montego van rear lights.

Rover, even though it was built on a near identical chassis. In fact, not only is the chassis borrowed from the RRC but the front bulkhead, windscreen, door frames, and the complete engine and transmission system is, too. Other parts came from the Rover parts bin, including Sherpa headlights, Metro indicator stalks, and Montego van rear lights, which all helped to bring production costs down.

The visual trick of making it look smaller was done by making the back door stop short of the rear bumper and sloping it forwards – it's not obvious but it actually slopes quite a lot. All this was done to combat the effect of the higher rear roof, designed to make it easy to get bicycles and other 'adventure' equipment in. It's also quite useful as a workhorse, too: with the rear seats out you can get a full-size standard industrial pallet in the back (as long as it goes in length ways), and the extra load height makes it possible to load it up using a small crane, too. The bodyshell has a welded-on steel roof and big rear pillars to give much

better roll-over protection than either the Range Rover or Defender, and it also has a welded-in steel rear floorpan, which all adds up to a much stronger shell. The downside is that all the extra steel adds weight, about 200kg of it, and most of it's quite high up. For that reason, early Discoveries tend to roll more in corners.

The rear roof height on Discoveries was needed to seat the rear passengers. The rear crossmember and boot floor are top rust spots.

Initially, the car had the 200Tdi (111bhp/195lbft) or 3.5-litre V8 (144bhp/192lbft) with twin carbs, LT77 five-speed manual, LT230 transfer box, and two-door body only.

In 1990, the four-door was launched, power windows became standard, and the V8 received fuel-injection (163bhp/212lbft). Over the following year there were gearbox changes to improve gear change on 1st and 2nd.

1992 saw the seven-seater renamed 'S,' central locking/alarm/immobiliser fitted as standard, and the ZF4HP22 four-speed automatic gearbox introduced. Exhaust catalysts were fitted to all petrol engines.

In 1993, the Rover four-cylinder petrol 2.0-litre Multi Port Injection (Mpi) engine (134bhp/137lbft) was introduced. A little underpowered for any hard work or towing but ok for light duty trips, it came about because some countries, such as Italy, had heavy taxes on vehicles over two litres. The Discovery Commercial was a very useful two-door car, without rear side windows, and employing a different floorpan at the back which extended further forward than the standard model. It was made to order by the Specialist Vehicles department.

The early Discoveries used Metro column switches; the dash switches could be operated without letting go of the steering wheel.

The V8 was enlarged to 3.9-litre (180bhp/230lbft) in 1994. Anti-roll bars were fitted front and rear, which reduced roll in corners very noticeably. Some earlier cars had roll bar mountings on the chassis but no bars were fitted, so these cars can be upgraded fairly easily.

A big change came later in 1994, when the 300 series face-lift arrived. The diesel engine was developed for better refinement. Named 300Tdi, it still produced 111bhp/195lbft, but was now attached to a new, stronger manual gearbox, the R380. The rear indicators were moved to the bumpers and the original position in the light cluster was taken up by a blank red panel, although the fitting for a bulb is still present. The bumper light units included the side and brake lights, to comply with new regulations that required the lights to

The 300-style Discovery gained brighter bespoke headlights and a host of mechanical and cosmetic improvements.

be visible when the rear door was open. The original side and brake lights were retained in the clusters, too, giving double the number of lights. Many people retrofitted the earlier rear light clusters so that the indicators would be doubled up, too, and Land Rover eventually made this arrangement standard in 1996. The headlights were enlarged from the original Sherpa units and were significantly brighter, although the 200-style lights were perfectly satisfactory if in good condition.

The interior was revised: the dash became clearer, and the heater became a dual-zone unit with rotary controls that were easier to use, and, more reliable, too. The front door storage bins were reversed and moved forward.

The top of the range model was now the ES with ABS, alloys, twin electric tilt and slide sunroofs, twin air-bags, and leather seats.

In 1995 the XS was introduced with new alloys, wheelarch extensions, and half-leather seats. The ES received powered seats. The following year there was a flurry of special editions – Argyll, Arden, and Aviemore – with different colours and trim that complemented the extensive model range, from the base Tdi/V8i, through S, GS, XS, to the top ES models.

The last year of production for the Discovery was 1998, when the Safari and 50th Anniversary models were introduced with similar spec to the XS. The following year, it was replaced by the Discovery 2 which, although very similar visually, was a totally different car: the axles were based on the new Range Rover P38a, the new chassis was wider, and the engines heavily revised.

Camel Trophy special editions were made from 1990 to 1997. All were used in the competition and have had a hard life, but were refurbished before being sold on and have a strong following which has boosted values. There are many replica cars, which are often in better condition than the real thing, but are worth considerably less. There's an official register of Camel Trophy cars which is very useful when trying to establish if a car is genuine. The cars had a full roll cage, large roof rack, front winch, and underbody protection, as well as many detail changes.

Honda made Discoveries for sale in Japan – exactly the same but called Honda Crossroads – and some have found their way to the UK.

DEFENDER

The Defender replaced the Series III in 1983, but initially was known only as '110' or '90' Land Rovers, the 'Defender' badge only arriving in 1990. Based on a RRC chassis that was either stretched to a 110in wheelbase or shrunk to 93in, and with unique outriggers and bracketry, the models had a distinctive Land Rover rear bumper/crossmember, and front bumper mounting points made to mimic the old Series design, allowing the fitment of Series bumper attachments. The Series III-based front

The coil-sprung chassis spawned the Land Rover replacement with the 110 in 1983.

bulkhead was carried over. In fact, most of the Defender bodywork was first put into production on the Series III-based 'Stage One,' but as the Range Rover axles are wider, the Defender needed wheelarch extensions as standard. The resulting iconic shape is a big attraction, and it looks like a Land Rover should – rugged and strong enough to tackle the harshest environments on the planet.

The 90 was introduced the following year. This is a later NAS V8 90 press picture showing the upmarket intentions of the brand. (Courtesy Land Rover PR)

The 110 was launched with 2.25-litre petrol and diesel engines from the Series III: Land Rover had traditionally used low-power and therefore low stressed engines that were very reliable and able to run on poor quality fuels. The following year, the 90 was launched with a 2.5-litre diesel (68bhp) derived from an old Series engine. Wind-up windows replaced the Series-style sliding windows on 110, and a low-power version of the V8 introduced on 110. There were a range of transmissions, with the Range Rover four-speed gearbox on V8 variants and the five-speed Rover LT77 on four-cylinder models. Allegedly, the five-speed was thought unable to cope with extreme off-roading, even though it was later used on the Range Rover.

The 127in wheelbase was also launched, and Special Vehicles department made a number of 6x6 versions.

The 127 was launched in 1985, using a cut-and-shut 110 chassis with 16in added in the middle. The five-speed LT85 Santana 'box was offered on V8 models, which were producing only 134bhp – this was an improvement on the first 110 V8, which managed only 114bhp so as to be 'safe' off-road.

In 1986, the diesel engine received a turbo, boosting power to 85bhp at the expense of reliability. The units were revised the following year, making them slightly more dependable.

The Defender name was introduced in 1990 as the Land Rover brand was being developed to cover all three models. The 127 became the 130, and, although the wheelbase remained the same, the chassis was now a purpose-built unit, no longer a cut-and-shut 110. Also that year, the 200Tdi diesel engine replaced the antiquated units.

The 300Tdi replaced the older variant in 1994, after only four years in production, and brought with it the R380 gearbox. After only another four years, this too was replaced; by the new TD5 five-cylinder common rail diesel engine, which offered stronger performance and huge tuning potential. This arrived in 1998, but military versions continued using the 300Tdi because of its easier servicing and resistance to electrical interference. The same year saw a 50th anniversary special edition featuring the Discovery 2 with 4.0-litre Rover V8, air-conditioning, and an auto gearbox.

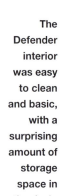

The Defender interior was easy to clean and basic, with a surprising amount of storage space in the dash.

The last incarnation of the original coil-sprung chassis. The Ford Transit-based engine and gearbox required a bonnet bulge.

A modified Defender featured in the film *Tomb Raider,* and in 2000 a special edition Tomb Raider model was released featuring dark metallic grey paint and an expedition-style roof rack.

In 2003, the company started selling G4 special editions with the same specification as the G4 international expedition vehicles, which included orange paint, front winch, and a roll cage.

A total rethink was needed as the TD5 reached the end of its life in 2007. Land Rover was part of Ford at the time so a suitable diesel engine and gearbox were sought from the existing Ford range. The Transit had recently received the new DuraTorq ZSD 2.4-litre diesel and six-speed MT82 gearbox, which seemed ideal for a hardworking Land Rover. Many modifications were required to be able to install the new engine in the car, most obviously the large bulge in the bonnet. The interior got its first big upgrade since the Series III in 1971: it used parts and gauges from the new Discovery 3 in a full width dash which rendered the iconic bulkhead vent flaps redundant; the

pattern is still visible in the metalwork but it's now a solid piece. The other big internal change was the replacement of the four rear inward facing seats, now outlawed in most countries, with two forward facing ones.

The SVX model marked the Land Rover 60th Anniversary in 2008. All were painted black with a distinctive new silver grille and headlamp surround, the main headlights incorporated the side lights, and the original side light spaces were filled with small high intensity driving lights – they also featured Recaro bucket seats and special alloy wheels.

Many other special editions and variations for individual markets have been made over the years: it's a characteristic of the company that it can make subtly new variants based on mixing and matching the large range of components available.

The Defender has also been made under licence by other companies around the world including: Santana in Spain; Otokar in Turkey; Karmann in Brazil; and Morattab in Iran using parts and tooling bought from Santana. Santana went on to design its own car,

which looks similar to a Defender but uses parabolic leaf springs and features a wider body with a full width rear door.

ALL MODELS
Body

All these Land Rovers are great for transporting the family, but, as mentioned earlier, because the rear wheelarch intrudes into the corner of the rear seat on Range Rover and Discovery models some child seats don't fit – just check the dimensions of the seat base before buying.

Discovery and Range Rover rear arches intrude into the rear seat sides, so not all child seats fit.

The welded joints at the top of the A- and B-pillars seem to be badly painted on some cars so check for corrosion here, as well as the bottom of the A-pillars where they join the floor.

The aluminium panels are fairly corrosion resistant, but where the metal has been exposed it will slowly turn to a white powder. The join between the steel frame and the outer ally side panels suffers from electrolytic corrosion where moisture gets trapped. Check the door bottoms, tailgate, and wing edges for blistering.

In the engine bay, check the inner wings, particularly where they meet the bulkhead and under the battery tray.

The front bulkhead, where it meets the sills and footwells, can accumulate dirt and moisture that makes the joint line rust out. Raise carpets and check for dampness and rust. Also check it from underneath; give the panels a good push and listen for crunching rust.

Sills rust at the rear edge where road grime is thrown at them by the rear wheels, the front of the sills may be rotten, too, particularly if the front mud flaps are missing. Range Rover and Discovery models have trim pieces that hide the rot so look carefully at the surrounding area for signs of spreading rust.

The other Discovery and Range Rover favourite rust spots; back of the sill, top of the arch, and the seatbelt mounts.

On four-door Range Rover and Discovery models, where the rear doors meet the wheelarch, there can often be trapped mud, leading to corrosion – pay particular attention to the rear seatbelt mounts. Also on these cars, the boot floor tended to rust due to moisture being trapped under the carpets, this is usually worst at the rear – lifting the mats up should reveal the extent of it.

On Discoveries the roof is steel and welded-on, sunroof leaks can make the upper surface of the headlining wet and cause the roof to rot from the inside.

Rear door locks seize-up due to lack of use; the aluminium corrodes and jams the latch in the raised position. (There's a very simple fix detailed in the repair chapter of this book.) In fact, all the door latch and lock mechanisms can get a bit stiff, making it difficult to open or lock doors, but it's all fairly easily fixed.

The window sealing strips perish, and cracks let in water which leads to corrosion in the panels below.

The Range Rover lower tailgate rusts at the bottom, as does the rear body crossmember that its hinges bolt to – lower the tailgate and lift the carpets to check for corrosion and moisture.

On Discoveries and Range Rovers, the jack and wheel chock should be found in the front nearside wing just behind the headlight. It rests on a rubber mat and is secured with a rubber strap. These parts can chafe away at the matting and erode the inner wing metal work, so it's worth removing them to have a good look at the steel.

Discoveries initially had the option of a soft 'handbag' in the centre console, in use it was secured with a clip on each side but it could be easily removed so you could take all your papers, CDs, and car sweets with you. Most of these have been lost over the years and replacements are getting rare.

Later models had a proper cubby box with a lockable lid – if you have one of these check there's a key for it.

Some Discoveries and later Range Rovers had a problem with parts of the dash peeling – repair kits are available.

Chassis

When checking out a potential new purchase, you have to get down and dirty. Look carefully under the middle of the chassis where the main crossmember is. This holds the top A-frame for the rear axle and is a prime target for rot. You might not be able to see it but reach up to the top surface and check for weak metal – be very careful as there could be very sharp exposed edges there.

The Defender rear bumper/crossmember traps water where it joins the main chassis rails, so have a good rummage round there. On Discovery and Range Rover models the rear crossmember is also prone to corrosion. It is hidden behind the rear bumper, making it difficult to inspect fully, but some of it can be seen from underneath.

Check the outriggers that secure the body: there are four main ones, a pair under the front bulkhead and a pair **just in front of the rear wheels. There are also smaller mounts at the rear and front**

On all models, rust attacks the chassis outriggers and sills (rockers). The main suspension bushes affect stability.

of the body, plus a myriad of smaller brackets.

Try to look at the top surface of the chassis rails on both sides of the car as they trap mud and corrode. Also check for off-road damage – scrapes on the chassis rails can rot through and seriously weaken the car.

Around 1989, the crossmember that supports the rear A-frame was improved; from the corrosion trapping squarish section unit to a more sensible round section tube.

Engine

The Rover V8 in 3.5-litre form was almost indestructible. It may leak oil from the valley gasket, rocker covers, and sump but that's fairly normal. It does need regular oil changes: many cars are neglected and driven far too long on old oil, which leads to tar build-up and possible big end bearing failure, cam wear, tappet collapse, rocker shaft wear, and worn bores. You must check an engine by starting from cold – when you view a car, open the bonnet and check the engine has not been warmed before you start it. Often engines are driven for years with less than the full eight cylinders working. Even when working badly, these tough little engines still work enough to drive the car, and that's the beauty of not being too highly tuned.

Water pump bearings wear, particularly if the car has ever lost coolant in its life. Look for tell-tale coolant traces on the back of the pump pulley.

When the bore was stretched for the 3.9- and 4.2-litre V, the cylinder liner was not held quite as well as the 3.5-litre engine: it has a tendency to creep down, which, in turn, compromises the cylinder head gasket clamping, and gasket leaks are very common. Engines with this fault are expensive to fix properly, although it has to be said the fault can usually be

'lived with' if not too severe. The results of this problem are a tendency to blow coolant out, resulting in overheating, and in some cases a tendency to burn a bit more oil than usual.

The 2.0-litre Mpi petrol used briefly in the Discovery was taken directly out of the Rover road cars. It's a simple and usually reliable engine, although performance is limited. A worn engine will make tell-tale rattling or tapping noises.

The VM diesel was an industrial engine with what can best be described as modest performance. It had individual cylinder heads on each cylinder and gaskets can give problems. The cost and rarity of parts makes repair less viable; in fact, if the engine has big problems then it may be cheaper to change it for a later Tdi engine.

200Tdi was the first decent performance diesel engine produced by Land Rover. It has proved very reliable if correctly maintained and can provide loyal service for a standard Landy; although tuneable, it has limitations and can be a bit noisy. Regular oil changes are essential to keep the turbo bearings in good order, and cam belt changes involve a large amount of work so ensure this has been done recently before you buy.

The 300Tdi replaced the 200Tdi around 1994; it's basically the same engine but with a large number of detail changes to make it more appealing. Firstly, it was quieter, with revised combustion chambers and fuel-injection equipment. Secondly, it was easier to work on, and the cam change requires much less work than on a 200Tdi – this was partly done to appease the British Army, who needed a simple and reliable unit that could be maintained easily in conflict zones. In fact, they liked the 300 so much that they kept ordering it even when it was replaced by the TD5

in mainstream cars. The 300Tdi engine initially had a reputation for misaligned timing belt followers, but all these will have been replaced when the belt was changed.

Regular timing belt changes are essential on both the 200 and 300Tdi – if there's no documented evidence that it has been changed recently then budget to do so as a precaution, they're not expensive and don't take very long to replace.

Check the turbo for oil leaks: if present then chances are oil has been spread all over the turbo, making it difficult to work out where it's leaking from. If the shaft seals have worn then oil may be present in the exhaust housing as well as the intake side, but if there's oil only in the intake side then it might be coming from the crank case vent system, possibly because of a worn engine. Unfortunately, you need to take the car apart to check this, but there's another clue when you start an engine from cold – if there's a large puff of blue or white smoke then this might be due to it burning off the puddle of oil.

The turbo will whistle quietly in operation. It shouldn't really be audible to bystanders but if it is then it may be because a hose has split, letting the air and sound out, or it might be because the turbo has become unbalanced due to damage. Never run a turbo without an air filter, the slightest bit of grit will damage it as it spins at over 120,000rpm.

The TD5 diesel was the first, and only, product from a new Rover modular engine design. The tooling was intended to produce four-, five-, and six-cylinder engines, but its launch coincided with the acquisition of Land Rover by BMW, which already had a 2-litre four pot and a 3-litre six-cylinder diesel engine. So only the TD5 was produced, although the names TD4 and TD6 were later used on vehicles with other engines.

The TD5 was another big step forward in technology: fully electronically controlled fuelling allowed the injectors to be switched off on overrun to save fuel (that's why the engine gets suddenly quieter when you back off the accelerator), it has greater tuning potential than the 300Tdi, and has been run in race vehicles at over 230bhp.

The unit has more complex oil filtering, to extend oil change intervals and improve oil quality for the more sensitive components. There's a conventional paper cartridge filter, plus an additional centrifugal filter with a central element that is spun at great speed by oil pressure – you can often hear it running down after you switch the engine off.

The 2.5-litre petrol was initially used in the Defender, and is an enlarged 2¼-litre, as seen in the Series III Land Rovers. It was simple but inefficient, providing very reliable service but very poor performance and economy.

Its cousin, the 2.5-litre diesel, used exactly the same block, but with different pistons and head. Again, it was very simple and reliable, but with even worse performance than the petrol, and only marginally improved economy. Later 2.5-litre TD versions were turbocharged to give a mild improvement in performance and economy, but with a reduction in reliability.

Puma is the name of the last diesel engine to be fitted to the Defender – it's the Ford Transit engine but with revised sump and oil pick up to cope with extreme tilt angles. It offers excellent economy and performance, and comes with a remarkable 'anti stall' system that has to be experienced to be believed. It's a very modern engine with extensive computer control of fuelling,

turbocharger, and cam timing. Servicing requires the use of a suitable computer diagnostic tool. It's a world away from the 200Tdi in all respects.

The alternator used on most models is a development of the old Lucas A127 unit, making it fairly simple for a specialist to rebuild. Alternator bearings will wear on high mileage cars or ones that have seen a lot of mud or wading.

Discoveries and models with the Tdi engines had a speed output from the back of the alternator to drive the rev counter, you can tell when it's not working well because the rev counter reading becomes erratic.

Cooling

Cooling problems usually occur because the radiator front face is blocked with debris, which can lead to the fins and cores corroding. Thermostats have been known to jam, so check any prospective purchase reaches normal operating temperature readily and doesn't overheat on a test drive. Because most engines are prone to oil leaks, coolant hoses can start to soften and rupture due to a coating of oil.

The visco fans fitted to most models become stiff when cold as they age so check the fan rotates easily with a cold engine. Stiff or seized fans rob power and economy.

Check the coolant level: a low level could be caused by a corroded radiator, a fractured heater matrix, leaking pipes, or even a leaking head gasket. The 3.9-litre V8 had a reputation for cylinder liners dropping, causing gasket failure and losing coolant. Check the coolant has antifreeze in by dipping a clean white rag or paper into the header tank. It should come out showing some colour (most coolants are blue, green, or red). If it shows clear water then

chances are the car regularly loses coolant and has been topped up with neat water.

Gearbox

The LT 77 five-speed manual suffers from wear in the input shaft bearing, which can result in: rumble and vibration when the clutch is pressed; oil leaking out of the bell housing; and eventual bearing collapse. Gear changes can be a bit slow but that's normal.

The new, heavily revised R380 version used the same casing but was entirely different inside. It's more robust, but suffers from loss of synchro in 2nd gear and a tendency not to allow swift changes up to 4th.

On diesel cars the vibration causes excessive wear on the gearbox output shaft, resulting in a delay when engaging drive and a thud as the slack is taken up.

Defenders had the option of the LT85 Santana gearbox, which is stronger but heavier, despite its aluminium casing.

The automatic Chrysler unit produces fairly abrupt gear changes as standard but is a durable unit. The later ZF 4HP22 should be very smooth in operation but high mileage units can suffer from rear clutch failure, which means they won't pull away in D, but will work normally in 1, 2, and 3, requiring an expensive repair. On both gearboxes the oil should be red – if it has turned brown then it's been overheated, indicating heavy wear and possible imminent failure. If the engine revs up before drive is engaged by the gearbox, or if it drops out of gear when cornering, the oil level maybe low. Leaking oil pipes may have perished and must be replaced.

The transfer box lever seldom gets used by most owners, so it's quite common for it to seize-up but it can usually be fixed fairly easily.

Axles

The early units used half shafts with 10 splines where they joined the differential. Although fine for normal use, these could break if frequently put under extreme load, so a slightly more robust 24 spline system was introduced in 1993. These later 'Fine Spline' axles can be interchanged for the earlier units if needed.

The introduction of ABS brakes in 1990 required a revised swivel pin bearing to reduce 'noise' in the system.

From 1989, some models had anti-roll bars, and the axles had mounting points welded-on.

Check the axles with one wheel raised on a suitable jack and the car safely chocked so the wheels can be rotated back and forth. Each wheel will rotate before the propshaft moves, however more than about 45 degrees indicates a heavily worn axle.

Propshaft UJ bearings wear if not regularly greased, resulting in speed related vibration, typically worst between 50 and 60mph.

Hub seals wear and let moisture in, which ruins the bearings. There have been a number of detail changes to hubs over the years with varying levels of success. In the worst case, a bearing will start to lock-up and spin its inner race on the hub shaft, resulting in it welding itself on and the wheel locking up.

Steering

The power steering box has a tendency to leak after a while, small leaks can be lived with but if it's dripping then the seals and bearings need to be checked and replaced where needed. Reconditioned boxes are readily available.

The power steering hoses become porous after about ten years.

Early Range Rovers have a box distinguishable by the three main bolts on the top, later cars had the four bolt design.

Brakes

Brakes are generally simple; discs all round for all models, except some Defenders which had drums at the back.

Later Defenders and all 110s had slightly bigger callipers, which can make a reasonable upgrade for other cars. Old pads can perish, particularly if the car has been wading – the friction material splits from the backing – so check when they were last changed. The brake fluid needs changing regularly on any car. The fluid in the reservoir should be clear or very light tan with most types of fluid, dark or grey fluid needs changing immediately.

Suspension

The car should sit level when parked. If it leans then a spring may have cracked or become weak. The bushes have a hard life, so look at the ones on the radius arms and if they're cracked or worn then

replacement is needed. Dampers are vital for good handling and safety; any oil leaks mean the unit has failed.

Air suspension vehicles should be able to run through all the height settings, raising and lowering, without tilting sideways.

Tyres

On road these cars are very sensitive to tyre condition, particularly on the rear axle which has a large influence on stability. Mismatched tyres are to be avoided. Check for cracking round the tread block bases and on the sidewalls, also check the date code (see chapter 8) to make sure the tyre is less than about six-years-old.

Identity

As with most cars, some are not what they pretend to be. A stolen car may have its identity changed simply by changing the number plates, so look at the cars documents – in the UK that is the V5, sometimes known as the log book – and check that the car has the right Vehicle Identification Number (VIN) stamped on the VIN plate riveted to the front of the engine bay above the radiator. However, this itself may have been swapped so it's vital to also check the VIN stamped into the chassis just in front of the right-hand spring hanger, and the engine number, too.

Chapter 6
Servicing

Land Rovers are very durable and can keep on running, albeit badly, despite very poor servicing. This unfortunately means that there are quite a few cars out there that are running very badly or in danger of imminent mechanical failure. A full service can transform a car by making the engine and gearbox smoother, reducing vibration, and improving fuel economy.

This chapter isn't a substitute for the correct workshop manual, but contains some of the tricks and tips that owners have picked up over the years. As such, it should be considered an addition to the standard manuals.

Grease the propshafts – in fact, do it right now! These are very often forgotten about and end up running dry, which leads to very rapid wear and potential failure. If a Universal Joint (UJ) fails then the propshaft can come free at one end

Older Land Rovers need regular maintenance; many parts are based on 1960s technology when it was expected that every car owner would spend the weekend tinkering under the bonnet.

There are many fluids to check, including gearbox and transfer box. The propshafts will vibrate at speed if not properly maintained.

and break into the body or push the car off the road.

Often, worn joints result in a rumble, vibration, or droning noise that is particularly bad at one road speed, usually between 50 and 70mph, depending on the length of the defective

The propshafts have three grease nipples each, which must be cleaned before attaching the grease gun to avoid pushing grit into the joints.

A typically worn swivel seal has stained the hub with oil. As well as letting oil out, it lets water in when wading.

shaft. If it's making a noise then the UJ bearings need replacing.

There's a grease point in each UJ, and also in each shaft for the sliding joint, so each prop has three greasing points – make sure they're all done.

The front hub swivels have a seal that's ground down by fine particles of grit in mud and road grime, which inevitably leads to them failing. Originally, the swivels contained gear oil to lubricate the Constant Velocity (CV) joint. A worn swivel seal will let this oil leak out and rapid CV wear follows. Later vehicles were supplied with a special grease instead of an oil, and, at the same time, the drain plug on the bottom of the swivel was deleted because the grease is assumed to last for as long as the CV, and would only be changed when the swivel is disassembled. This 'One Shot' grease can be retrofitted to older cars once the old oil has been drained out, and means that no further servicing is needed.

However, while a worn swivel seal will not let the grease leak out, it will unfortunately let water in when wading. For this reason, the seal must be kept in good condition.

The front and rear hub seals are of variable quality, and after wading water

may have been drawn past the seal into the wheel bearing area. If the wading is brief and followed by a long run, the water drawn in may be minimal and evaporate readily, but often the bearing grease will be contaminated and, if unchecked, the bearing will wear over the following few months.

The stub axle, seen here after the seal had perished and the car was taken wading – water got in and wrecked the bearings.

After wading it's wise to remove the wheel hubs and check the grease is OK. If there's evidence of water ingress then clean the bearing and pack with fresh grease.

A failing wheel bearing may continue to appear to work

This 22-year old RRC chassis shows typical surface rust spots spreading like measles. Where water is trapped the rot goes straight through.

for some time. There may be some rumble at speed but it's not always noticeable. The rollers in the bearing become smaller and the races wear until eventually a roller can dislodge from the cage and jam in the bearing sideways. This results in the inner race of the bearing spinning on the stub axle, getting hotter until it welds on solidly, and the wheel will lock-up. Obviously, this is extremely dangerous so checking the bearings should be part of your regular maintenance schedule. If the bearing does weld onto the stub axle a new stub will need to be fitted.

A word of warning: the later Range Rovers with air suspension should not be lifted on two-post ramps, or by any other means that leaves the axles dangling, as this will stretch the air-bags and has been known to result in the rubber tearing. Always ensure the axles' weight is taken by suitable stands when working on a raised vehicle.

Old Land Rovers leak oil, fact. This usually means the front half of the chassis is well protected from rust by a thick layer of oil, but the rear half often suffers terribly. Areas such as the crossmember where the rear A-frame mounts are, tend to trap moisture and mud. So when cleaning off after off-roading ensure that all debris is blown clear from these areas, including

the top of the main chassis rails where the small gap between chassis and body can trap clods of dirt.

Areas on the chassis under the most stress tend to rust first, so inspect the body mounts, rear crossmember, and spring seats which often start rusting along the welds.

The chassis can be protected with chassis sealant but the metal underneath must be rust and dirt free before applying, otherwise the rot will be trapped under the sealant and corrode through. Often on off-road courses parts of the chassis will be scratched and the under seal damaged, so as part of the servicing regularly apply a little light oil to the welds and scratches, then yearly redo the under seal. If the car is going to be used off-road then chassis maintenance has to be considered a regular task.

On Range Rovers and Discoveries the rear seats can be removed to provide much greater load space. There are four small bolts holding each part of the rear seat to the car floor, and these secure a clamp bracket which houses a plastic bush to allow the front support tube of the seat to hinge forwards. Unfortunately, as these bolts protrude to the underside of the body, they're exposed to road grime and corrosion. So if you are thinking of taking the seats out on a regular basis it's worth replacing these bolts with stainless cap head bolts and keeping them lubricated.

All V8 engines need frequent oil changes, which can often be forgotten about. This neglect causes tar to build up in the oil galleries and clog the valve gear, resulting in rapid rocker shaft wear and possible failure of cam followers, which, in turn, reduces power and makes a heavy tapping noise. There have been plenty of cases of cars being driven in this condition with the owners blissfully unaware of the damage. In

The V8 can still run even when a couple of cylinders are not working, so, all too often, unconscientious owners can't be bothered servicing or fixing faults.

more severe cases, the oil feed to the main bearings can be compromised and failure becomes inevitable. If you have just bought a car and the oil is in poor condition then change it immediately. Drive the car normally for a few hundred miles so the detergents remove the deposits and then change it again. The oil filter must be changed on both occasions, too.

The V8 engine on the later 3.5-litre and all larger capacities has an idle speed control valve at the back of the plenum chamber which can get clogged with oil and tar. This results in an unstable idle speed and stalling as the

The later V8 idle speed control valve gums up, and can result in the engine stalling. A quick clean-up, and normal service is resumed.

valve fights against the blockage. To prevent this, remove the valve and clean off the gunge with WD40, or similar. There may be deposits stuck inside the valve so it may be necessary to repeat the cleaning process.

The distributor cap tends to foul-up the terminals with a hard white deposit, which can cause the engine to lose power and stall at idle. If this happens when out in the wilds, simply scrape the deposits off with the edge of a coin. Dressing the terminals with a small grinding tool will restore them briefly but, as the corrosion eats into the terminals and widens the spark gap, the cap will eventually need to be replaced.

The Tdi engines have a cam belt that must be replaced as recommended in the manual. However, using the car in wet and hot conditions increases wear in the belt and more frequent changes are required. Being rubber, the belt ages even when not in use. If the car is a Play Day toy then change the belt yearly at least.

The cam belt has a tensioning pulley and early ones had a tendency to fail – these can be replaced by the later unit. The idler is designed to be changed with every belt change, so don't just change the belt on its own.

During a maintenance inspection, remove the sound deadening cover and check the wiring and hoses are not chafing. One of the top failure areas occurs on 300Tdi engines where a small cooling hose rubs on the fan belt pulley – it needs to be clipped back.

Some of the hose clearances are very small, and some hoses may end up rubbing until they fail. The top suspects here are the bottom hose rubbing on the steering box, and the 300Tdi top heater hose rubbing on the fan belt. If your car has this problem then the hose may need re-orientating and supporting with wide cable ties, or to be replaced.

Another problem is mud blocking the radiator, particularly on models with an air-conditioning radiator in front of the engine radiator, which traps debris between the two. Be gentle when cleaning it: get baked on mud very wet before trying to remove it with a soft brush, using water from a hose not a pressure washer, which can damage the fins.

The transfer box lever can seize-up. Often, it can be brought back to life with a bit of wiggling, but stubborn items may need to be lubricated from underneath the car, and in severe cases the linkage must be striped down and rebuilt.

The rubber seals on sunroofs age faster than other rubber parts due to more direct contact with sunlight. As they harden or crack they start leaking water into the headlining, so keep them supple by wiping with silicone grease.

On all models, the hazard light switch can stop working because it never gets used and the contacts tarnish. So before the car's annual test, just operate the switch several times until it starts working properly.

There are many electrical connectors in the engine bay prone to corrosion. Check them and, if in good condition, coat with spray grease to provide long-term protection. If already corroded, fit new connectors to avoid systems failing when the car is miles from help.

Door locks must be lubricated and operated regularly. Many later cars have remote locking so the key lock in the door may not get used for years, which often results in it seizing.

The rear door handle on Discoveries can corrode and seize-up: lubricate with spray oil such as WD40 to avoid this.

Windscreen wipers have a hard life. Scraping the blade across a screen covered in mud or grime wears the edge very quickly, so always use the washer jets on the first wipe. In winter, if the blades have frozen to the screen, wait until the heater has defrosted them before using them, and never pull them off a frozen screen or the blade edge will be damaged.

Mud contains fine grit particles and using the wipers to clear a muddy screen not only damages the wipers but rubs this grit across the window; just like sand paper, it scratches the glass. So, again, use the washer jets extensively, or if there's a lot of mud stop and remove it manually before continuing on.

Eventually the screen will become scratched, which makes it harder for the wipers to remove rain water and can cause blurring of lights at night. These micro scratches can be removed by polishing with domestic glass polish and lots of hard rubbing.

The transfer box control lever is often left unused by many owners, resulting in the linkages seizing. Usually, a good strong wiggle on the lever starts to free it.

After checking all the electrical connections were in good order, these connector blocks in the engine bay have been protected with contact grease spray.

The rubber sunroof seals can become hard and brittle, which results in leaks. This ancient seal is still working, due to being protected with a smear of silicone grease.

All the door locks need lubrication, particularly the ones not used often. This Discovery rear door latch had seized, but with a little wiggling and some oil it came back to life.

Wipers on muddy screens result in fine scratches. Sometimes these can be polished out with domestic glass polish and a lot of elbow grease!

To stop the wipers and jets freezing on very cold journeys increase the screen wash concentration significantly.

The bonnet release also needs lubrication, and is often forgotten. The cable and latch are right at the front and get blasted with rain and grime, which can remove the grease and start corrosion.

Tyre technology has moved on in recent years, which makes some of the tyre pressure reconsiderations in the official books obsolete. Tyre pressure has a profound effect on handling, grip, and safety, both on and off-road. Check pressures regularly and adjust to suit the job the car is being used for – just like any other tool, they have to be set up correctly. Generally, road work needs a higher pressure than off-road work. Some tyres work very well at pressures above 40psi, others have a maximum of only 30psi, while some off-road situations may need as little as 15psi. The safest course of action is to consult the tyre manufacturer – explain what you are doing and they will be able to make sound suggestions that could transform the cars handling.

Tyres are the most critical part of the car, but often get neglected. Correct pressures depend on the conditions and load carried.

LAY UP AND RECOMMISSIONING

Many of these cars will be left standing unused for long periods, which can significantly increase corrosion rates. Over long periods, the oil film will completely drain from engine parts, gears, and differentials, exposing metal to moist air. Many of these parts have a very thin surface hardening, and when corrosion takes hold this layer can be ruined very easily, leading to rapid wear next time the car is used.

Peering into the murky depths of an R380 gearbox shows the cogs glistening with the protective oil film. This oil drains away if the car is left standing, which can result in rust.

This means a car must be driven regularly during the lay up period, even if only for a short distance. When a cold engine is started, water condenses out of the exhaust gasses and pools in the exhaust system. As the exhaust pipe heats up it eventually gets hot enough for the water to evaporate, resulting in a temporary increase in the amount of white vapour coming out of the tail pipe. It's important to keep the engine running until this phase has finished because stopping the engine before the pooled water has been driven out will rapidly increase exhaust corrosion. If it's not possible to run the engine then it could have a few drops of oil left in the bores, which should be dispelled by cranking over with the plugs out when recommissioning. There are lay up oils and additives which drain less readily for engine and gear parts, these should be replaced with normal oils before recommissioning.

Moisture being driven out of a warming exhaust on a hot day may only show as a faint haze. On a cold day it will be a clearly visible white vapour.

Killer weeds. Grassy parking spots trap moisture, and the underside of the car will suffer if left for long periods.

Brake pads can slowly bond onto the discs, and handbrake shoes can bond onto the drum. This means it will feel as though the brakes are on but they will suddenly free-off when pulling away. Unfortunately, in doing so, they will have lost some of their integrity and may fail soon afterwards.

Moisture will condense on metal panels every day as the temperature rises and falls. In normal use, driving will draw air through the car, removing the moisture. During lay up moisture will simply accumulate in cavities and floor mats. To prevent this ensure the storage area has some air flow through and is protected from rain. Avoid storing cars on grass or dirt, which generates huge amounts of moisture and will rot the underside of a car very rapidly.

AGEING

Many parts age, even when not in use; most notably rubber, which reacts with oxygen in the air to become hard and brittle. Sunlight speeds up this process and tyres stored in the open will crack within a few years. But even hidden parts, such as cooling hoses and fuel pipes made of rubber, will perish. Ten years should be considered the maximum life of a rubber component, and six years the maximum life of a tyre, regardless of tread depth. Fuel pipes should be replaced for safety well before they show clear signs of perishing.

Engine coolant (antifreeze) gradually becomes acidic and must be replaced after about three years,

The oil condition can be tested on special paper cards that let the drop of oil spread out into its component parts.

otherwise it will slowly start eating away at the cooling system and engine from within.

Mileage cannot be considered the only indicator that oil replacement is necessary. Oil ages and should be replaced every year, even if mileage is minimal. Oils also age whilst still in the can: additives separate out and form a jelly-like substance in the bottom of the can. When this happens the oil is no longer usable.

Brake fluid absorbs moisture. Sold in sealed containers, it starts to age as soon as the seal is broken, and must be discarded after a time – just as if it was in the car.

Fuel ages too, more so with modern complex blends. The lighter parts of petrol evaporate and leave a thick lacquer which can jam injectors and fuel pumps. If the car is to be laid up for a long period, fuel stabiliser fluids can be added to the tank.

Brake pads perish, and the bond between the friction material and the metal backing plate can crack, resulting in the pad failing. Often, the pads will work fine until the bond breaks entirely and the friction material completely falls out. The next time the brakes are used the pedal will travel a long way

as the calliper piston pushes the bare backing plate into the disc. The brake will appear to work again, but with a scraping noise from the metal to metal contact. However, in an emergency stop the car will veer sideways, before the backing plate is ejected, the piston falls out of the calliper, and all braking is lost. For this reason, inspect the bond on the brake pads very carefully, and replace them before they perish.

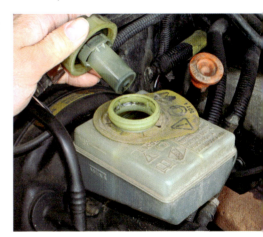

Brake fluid can turn dark grey as it ages. If it looks this black, the car is at serious risk from brake fade under heavy braking.

Look closely and the tiny crack between the friction material and the metal backing on this old brake pad is visible. The other pad on this calliper completely lost its friction material during an emergency stop.

Door-mounted spare tyres receive higher levels of UV, and can perish even faster than the ones on the road. Spare wheel covers can help.

All rubber parts perish; these rear damper bushes have all but disintegrated whilst hidden from view, making handling feel slack.

Chapter 7
Repair

Some repair jobs are bigger than others.

Most repair operations are well described in the relevant manuals, but occasionally there are problems that were not thought of when the original texts were written. Additionally, years of driving experience by millions of owners have thrown up some unusual quirks, and also some handy tricks for diagnosing and fixing them.

So this chapter is designed to supplement a standard workshop manual; to spread some of the knowledge, the things 'they' don't tell you – gained the hard way.

BODYWORK

Before welding bodywork, ensure that all trim and wiring is removed from the area where heat and weld spatter may fall. Ensure all repairs are done to the highest standard so that the body remains strong; just think about what happens in the event of a crash – it could be a matter of life and death.

The sills support the A-, B-, and C/D-pillars and, as such, hold the body together. In a side impact they're vital for your survival, so it's rather unfortunate that they're one of the top rust traps. There are two approaches to repair: the usual method is to cut out the old sill and weld in a new piece (ready made repair sections are readily available and make the job a lot easier); the other is to replace it with something stronger, such as a heavy gauge box section,

This Range Rover had a new rear arch panel welded-in, but, unfortunately, the sill end was not properly repaired and has completely rotted away under the plastic trim.

which, if tied into the body mounting points, means you can then jack the car up on the sills – a very useful technique in some off-road situations. For more information see 'Jackable sills' in the Modification chapter.

The Range Rover top tailgate rots wherever steel meets aluminium, and, being quite spindly, it's not easy to

The rear body crossmember on this Range Rover has rotted out completely, and the tailgate hinge has come free. Luckily, preformed repair sections are readily available to weld in.

repair. Small rot spots can be cleaned up and filled with a strong resin to rebuild some strength, but the tailgate usually needs to be replaced. Luckily, there are a few companies making new replacement parts.

The lock mechanism often seizes up: it's at a slight angle and fills up with water. It can be rejuvenated by stripping down and cleaning, but if it's too far gone then a new lock can be fitted. The lock barrels can be swapped over so you don't end up with odd keys.

The lower tailgate rots from the bottom up, and the hinges are a prime target so need to be kept well lubricated. The frame is usually fairly sound, but the outer skin does rust from the lower edge. If so, it's possible to cut the affected area out and weld in a new section of flat steel. Another option is to cut out the rust, treat the edges, then bolt on an ally cover plate, which if done well can look quite good. Whichever method is used, make sure the drain holes are preserved, otherwise moisture builds back up and the bottom will rot out again.

Range Rover models with the Webasto full length sunroof suffered from corrosion where seals began letting rain in. Light corrosion can be treated

and the fabric repaired or replaced, but many have gone too far and will have to be completely replaced. Unfortunately, parts are very rare, and it may be more pragmatic to replace the whole roof with a standard item. But whilst the roof is a simple bolt-on unit, the steel frame it bolts to was slightly different on Webasto models, and, as such, the rail above the windscreen must be altered or replaced.

The C channel that holds the door glass in the lift mechanism has a tendency to rust and lose grip of the glass – often the window will still go up and down but may make a crunching sound and may drop in a jerky or sudden way. It's possible to fit a new C section to the glass, but it's very difficult to get the right clamping load to make a durable repair so it's often easier to fit a good secondhand glass assembly.

Range Rover top tailgates are another top rot spot, so check the hinge area and bolts. New parts are readily available.

Fitting the glass requires the removal of the door card and the window frame. When refitting the frame after the glass has been inserted, it must be adjusted to fit snugly against the door seal to avoid gaps and increased road noise. This can be a bit tricky but a good method is to bolt the frame in loosely before closing the door to get a rough starting point, then open the door and adjust the frame inward, very slightly tighten the bolts, and recheck.

The Classic tailgate rots from the lower edge up. Patches can be welded-in, but another option is to cut out the rot and plate over the whole area in ally.

Front inner wings on all models are flat steel sheets that corrode where mud and moisture accumulates on the flat top and at the bulkhead joint. Repair panels are available, although they're simple to fabricate from flat sheet. If the joint at the bulkhead is corroded, a sheet may be needed to repair the bulkhead before commencing on the inner wing.

Discovery and Range Rover rear inner wings and seatbelt anchors are a top rot spot. A repair section is

The window frame bolts allow a large variation in position, but the frame must sit firmly against the door seal to avoid wind noise.

The inner wing is made of flat panels that can hold mud and water. They have little structural strength and can be easily fabricated in steel or aluminium.

Often rust grows where the wing bolts onto the inner wing upper edge. Moisture trapped in the footwell edges and headlight cowl can corrode the edges. They can usually be repaired with an angled steel strip.

available which replaces the outer part of the arch; the old arch is cut at the junction of the rear wing and at the sill, then along the arch seam. Welding near the rear wing is problematical due to the proximity of the aluminium panel. If there's insufficient bare metal available in front of the wing, the wing must be released and held away from the join area. These repair sections do not include the seatbelt mounting area, which has to be a sound and solid piece of metal, so great care is needed in repairing it. Cut the surrounding metal back to full thickness sound metal and fit a sheet of the same strength as the original to the underside of the area – so that in an accident it would have to pull through the floor to fail. Attach a replacement strengthening piece under the mounting point to spread the load, as per original design.

Discovery and Range Rover boot floors suffered from moisture collecting under the matting and corroding it, mainly around the joints. Early cars had a corrugated aluminium floor that was bolted in and corrosion badly affected the bolts and captive nuts, often

dissolving the whole area. If refitting a new aluminium floor, the steel bodywork may have to be repaired first, and new captive nuts welded-in. Later steel floors are welded-in, and, again, some repair to the surrounding steel work may be needed. In both cases, the floor is joined to the chassis via two small adjustable mountings that incorporate the inner two rear seatbelt mounts. The mounting bolts that go through the belt mounts may be heavily corroded underneath, where exposed to road grime, so will need to be cleaned up and lubricated before attempting to undo. Extreme caution is needed when working in this area as the fuel tank is directly below, so only professionals should attempt repairs here.

The Defender bulkhead is basically the same as those found on old Series Land Rovers, and suffers corrosion at every panel joint. There comes a time where patching it up again becomes impractical, so replacing the whole thing starts to make sense. Although it's obviously a big job, it's reasonably straightforward. Start by unbolting the roof, bonnet, and front wings, then

The top rot spots on Range Rovers and Discoveries are the seams in the wheel arch and the rear seatbelt mounting point. This repair panel only fixes the outer arch.

remove the screen. Take the doors off and undo everything attached to it, such as the pedal box and instrument pod etc. The old bulkhead is cut from the floor, ensuring enough material is left for a strong weld base – the floor may need to be repaired with flat sheet before going further. Getting the replacement bulkhead to align with everything is a complex task, and, if possible, a jig should be made prior to removal of the old bulkhead that bolts to the seat bases, or other suitable points, and locates onto at least three of the bulkhead's main features, such as door hinge location points and steering column mounting points. The jig must be triangulated so as not to move when the bulkhead is removed. The alternative method is to offer up the new bulkhead and loosely bolt on the roof, doors, and wings to check everything aligns. In both cases, the reference dimensions quoted in the official repair manual should be measured and adhered to before final welding.

The Defender roof can leak where the seal between the roof and the windscreen top has hardened and cracked, resulting in water getting in and pooling in the front footwells. There are two ways of fixing this: first is to remove the headlining and run a bead of sealant round the joint, but a better solution is to remove the roof and fit a new seal.

Load beds rust from where the strengthening rib is welded-on underneath, and from the rear edge under the plastic trim.

As mentioned in the previous chapter, a common problem on older Discoveries is a tendency for the rear door release handle to stick in the up position, rendering the door un-openable. Often this fault is misinterpreted as a sticking lock, but it's one of the simplest problems to fix. What happens is the aluminium release

Defender Bulkheads frequently rust on the seams but are bolt-on assemblies, so swapping in a new one is relatively straightforward.

handle corrodes slightly, and it's this white powdery aluminium corrosion that jams the handle in its housing. An effective temporary solution is to prise the Land Rover logo off to gain access to the back of the handle, spray releasing oil such as WD40 on the edges of the handle, and once it has soaked in simply press the handle back down. Operate the handle, pushing it fully up and down, several times whilst giving it another dose of oil. It should then feel free and work properly again. If it's still sticky then it needs removing and stripping down to clean it up properly, then repaint the parts before reassembling.

One of the more common failures is the rear seat back hinges on Discovery and late Range Rover models coming undone. The hinge consists of a domed head hex drive bolt and a small collar, which allows one part of the hinge to rotate freely about the other. After many years of service the bolts work loose and fall out, although it's quite simple to replace them and return the seat to service.

The rear window washer jet on Discoveries often comes loose because

Defender roof leaks are usually due to hardening of the seal on the screen top. Remove the headlining to check for telltale water marks.

The discovery rear door handle can seize; the badge pops out to give access to the moving parts.

one of its plastic locating lugs has broken. Fitting a new one is just a matter of pressing it in, but before removing the old unit secure the water tube; if it falls back into the car then the rear interior trim has to be removed to get it out. Gently pull the old unit away, and tape the tube to the car before removing it from the washer jet. The part number is PRC6496, fit it by twisting 90 degrees.

CHASSIS

If a number of chassis repairs are needed it may prove easier and safer to fit a replacement chassis.

The chassis twists and bends during off-road manoeuvres, and it has to put up with huge forces, so any repairs must be of the highest quality.

Any welds must be professionally done, so if your skills are anything other than perfect, get the professionals in.

It's interesting to note that the front sections of the chassis are usually well protected from corrosion by the many oil leaks that seem to come as standard. Often from the transfer box forward there's a thick coating of black oil. The transmission, engine, front diff, and power steering system all contribute to this phenomenon.

Ironically, well-maintained, leak free cars suffer from the worst chassis rot, although the rear section suffers terribly from rust on all cars. On early

Discovery and Range Rover rear seat brackets come undone. They use a short bolt and a spacer tube to form the hinge.

The front of this Range Rover chassis and axle are clearly benefiting from the oil leak rust protection system!

Rear chassis rot often needs major surgery. (Courtesy Devon 4x4)

chassis the crossmember that mounts the rear A-frame has a flat top surface that traps mud and wet road grime. It's quite difficult to get at and is often missed on inspections, so the rot starts at the top and spreads down until it becomes obvious from the underside. It's made from thick steel and often there's enough remaining material to allow new metal to be welded-in. Although, if the rot has gone all the way round the crossmember the best bet is to cut it out completely and weld in a replacement. Later chassis use a tubular crossmember which avoids the mud trap, and this can be used as a replacement for earlier items. It must be fitted accurately to ensure the A-frame geometry is maintained, otherwise the handling could be dangerously compromised. Making a simple jig that locates the mounting points is a good idea. This could be a bar, tack-welded across the chassis above the crossmember, with pieces descending down that bolt to the mounting points. Fitted before cutting out the original crossmember, this will help ensure the mounting points will be in exactly the same place. In fact, making little jigs like this is good practice on any areas of chassis repair involving mounting points.

The rear crossmember also

Rear chassis showing widespread rust; the top of the square section crossmember above the A-frame is completely corroded.

This chassis is relatively good, but rust is just starting on all the seams. Rear crossmembers rust behind the bumper.

corrodes. Road grime is thrown at it and mud gets trapped on the upper surface of Range Rover and Discovery items. Defender items have a number of rust traps, and rot from the inside out. In both cases, new rear crossmembers are available, which can be welded-in. If you need to do this it may be worth considering uprated items.

The outriggers that support the body also have flat upper surfaces that trap wet mud. Again, new repair sections are available and can be welded-in. Before cutting the old outrigger out, the chassis and body must be well supported to stop them moving relative to each other. To ensure the new item is located accurately, the body mounting can be temporarily reassembled before welding the outrigger to the chassis.

Any welding on the main chassis will burn off the protective paint on the inside and promote rust. After any such repair the chassis should be sprayed internally with paint via a flexible nozzle, or with a wax-based sealant.

It's worth noting that many chassis will have been wax treated at some point and welding the chassis can actually set fire to the wax inside the chassis rails.

Body support outriggers can be cut out and replaced. Discovery and Range Rover body mounts like this use isolating rubbers.

This removable crossmember was left bolted in when the chassis was galvanised, so it was almost impossible to remove and the joining face was left untreated.

The two jack method of aligning the crossmember.

Removing the central bolt-in crossmember can be made easier by securing a high lift jack between the chassis rails and easing them very slightly apart. Never work under the jack as it can fall and cause serious injury.

Front damper towers rust at the top and bottom. Luckily, these are simple bolt-on items, but the mounting bolts that are welded onto their own mounting ring corrode and often need replacing at the same time. There are a number of alternative damper mountings available: see the Modification chapter for more information.

Rear damper mounts are bolted in, but rust can form between the mount and chassis to weaken this critical area. Again, the chassis must be repaired

The bolt-in crossmember goes under the gearbox; one of the bolts on each side goes into the body support outrigger.

properly to remain strong enough for its purpose.

Spring mounts have a hard life: grime trapped where the spring meets the mount is constantly ground in, and the stress where the mount is welded to the chassis results in corrosion. This usually means that if the mount needs replacing then that area of the chassis needs repairing, too. It must be cut back to good sound metal, and a strengthening plate welded-on, before the new spring mount is attached.

MECHANICAL

The differential input shaft oil seal is a substantial item with a steel collar that is press fitted into the diff housing. It's always troublesome to remove, due to it being so far inside the housing, and there's a special hook shaped tool available for this job. The alternative is to collapse the collar by driving a slim chisel between it and the housing without damaging the bore, but it's definitely not easy!

If the car makes a knocking noise when turning tight corners then chances are the CV joint on the front axle has broken. If unchecked, the parts will break up and could seize, dangerously locking the wheel.

Front damper turrets rust at their base and at the recessed top. Often the bolts will have to be cut off due to corrosion.

Rear spring and damper mounts can rust at the chassis joint, requiring repairs to the chassis to regain strength.

An LT230 transfer box showing the linkages to the high/low range and diff lock, which can become very stiff if rarely used.

Luckily, it's fairly simple to fix: remove the brake calliper, remove the hub and stub axle, and the CV is right there. Slide it carefully off the half shaft in case there are any loose bits. If it has broken up, all the debris has to be removed from the axle to avoid it causing further damage.

If you can't engage low range, the most common cause is the lever mechanism getting stiff with old mud and grit. The first step is to try moving the lever back and forth several times to see if it starts to free up as it knocks the dirt off. The next step is to get

New propshaft bearings slip on and are retained by circlips. If grease emerges when filling, the rubber seals need replacing.

Wider yokes allow greater articulation for long travel suspension.
(Courtesy Devon 4x4)

underneath and wash the grime off the mechanism, from the lever to the rod on the transfer box. Sometimes bits of gravel get lodged on top of the transfer box where the lever goes in, so check this area carefully. Once it's clean give it a good dose of light oil, then try moving the lever again.

Vibration at somewhere between 50 and 70mph has many possible causes, such as imbalanced wheels or worn or badly adjusted differentials, but one of the most common causes are the propshafts. The UJ bearings wear out and suffer very badly from lack of greasing if the maintenance has been skimped. The longer prop vibrates at a lower speed, interestingly. To check them, first chock the car safely, release the handbrake and put it in neutral, then give the props a good wiggle.

Vibration when changing gear is a particular problem on diesels: it wears the splines on the input shaft so when the clutch is dipped it all gets a bit slack.

The solution would be to fit a new input shaft, but this is a big job and it might be cheaper to fit a secondhand gearbox instead. Don't ignore the problem though – when it finally wears through the splines you suddenly get no drive at all, usually when you are pulling out of a busy junction in the rain at rush hour!

If you find that on long journeys the clutch pedal sometimes travels down on is own, making gear changes awkward, but pumps up again quite easily, then chances are it has an internal fault in the master cylinder. A very small number of these appear to be prone to this behaviour, and the best cause of action is to fit a new one.

EXHAUST

It's quite common for the welds in mild steel systems to rot out – wading and playing in mud speeds this up considerably. Small holes can be patched with exhaust seal tape, although this tends to work loose and is susceptible to damage off-road. A better solution is to weld a patch of steel sheet over the fault, where possible.

Eventually the faulty exhaust must be replaced, at which point the sleeve-type joints will refuse to budge. When this happens, the faulty part can be cut near the joint, and the remainder stuck in the joint persuaded out with a hammer and chisel. However, on cars with catalysts, restraint must be applied. Catalysts are very susceptible to damage from hammering so, if retaining

Impressive corrosion along the tube seam on a Range Rover exhaust.

Soot on the exhaust gasket indicates a leak. On fuel-injected cars with oxygen sensors, this will cause the engine to run rich and increase fuel consumption.

Inserting a new exhaust system is much easier if the car is raised slightly to provide a larger gap between the axle and body.

blanking plate instead, which is usually a lot easier and the loss in theoretical efficiency is quite small.

COOLING

Most of these cars are well over ten-years-old now, and the cooling system suffers from age quite badly. All the rubber bits perish, and it's best to replace them every ten years. The hose clips also corrode and should be renewed at the same time. Coolant becomes acidic over time and should be replaced every three years, and the water it's mixed with should be mineral free rather than just tap water. Trouble is, many owners just simply don't do this, so the coolant becomes corrosive, the hoses start to leak, and the system is topped up with tap water, resulting in scale deposits – just like in your kettle at home.

The white deposits on this thermostat housing are due to aluminium corrosion leaching out from underneath the top hose.

the catalyst section, avoid heavy shocks that might fracture the ceramic catalyst brick. Also, when removing cats from the manifold it's vital to prevent any particles of gasket or dirt entering the catalyst: even tiny pieces will rattle round and gradually erode the catalyst surface. When refitting catalysts to the manifold, new gaskets should be used – used gaskets are already crushed up and will not seal the joint fully. Gasket sealant paste should be avoided due to the risk of it falling in to the catalyst or contaminating the oxygen sensor.

The upstream gaskets, which are the ones between the catalyst and manifold, and the ones between the manifold and cylinder head, must be absolutely gas tight. Even a small leak draws air in, which results in the oxygen sensor reading lean. This causes the engine to run excessively rich.

The rear section of the exhaust extends over the rear axle and is almost impossible to remove, unless the car is raised to allow the axle to drop sufficiently.

On any modified vehicle, there's a

higher chance that the exhaust will have to be taken apart again at a later date for further modification, so a little copper grease on sleeve joints and sealing rings will make life easier further down the line.

The Exhaust Gas Recirculation (EGR) valve has a slightly unfair reputation. The idea is that as exhaust gas is inert, introducing a small amount into the intake slightly cools combustion and also improves efficiency. What that means is that the mpg is improved by up to five per cent and emissions of Nitrogen oxides are drastically reduced. The valve is controlled to give peak efficiency at part load and shut off when you put your foot down. The trouble is that the valve has to cope with very hot gas containing soot and corrosive nasties and can jam up, which results in recirculation at full load and causes excessive exhaust smoke and poor economy. It can sometimes be brought back to life by removal and cleaning, but if it's very clogged then it might need replacement. Another solution is to remove it permanently and fit a

If the system starts to leak, some people put in a chemical cooling system sealer, just poured from the bottle into the header tank. Whilst this stops the leak, it also coats the inner galleries of the cylinder head, radiator, and heater matrix, and, in the worst cases, causes engine overheating or a cold running interior heater. So if the radiator or heater matrix is leaking take it out and get it properly repaired or, better still, re-cored.

On older cars it's usually worth flushing the system through and replacing the perishable parts. Those hoses can look ok from the outside but its inner layer can collapse, restricting flow and causing the engine to overheat when under load. So give them a squeeze (not when hot) and search for unusually soft spots. The internal reinforcement fabric (either string or Kevlar) can fail, causing the hose to bulge out when under pressure.

The radiator suffers from corrosion from road salt, which can cause the delicate fins to become detached from the core tubes. This ruins its ability to transfer engine heat to the cooling air flow, so must be repaired immediately.

Radiator cores have a hard life. The fine fins are attacked by everything that hits the front of the car, and can easily become blocked by mud.

The thermostat can fail: if it's shut the engine overheats very rapidly, if it's open it never warms up. Although it can fail with age, and there's also some very poor fake parts in circulation, too, the most common reason for thermostat failure is overheating caused by some other fault. So if the thermostat has failed, check the rest of the system, the fan, and head gaskets, too.

The engine core plugs also corrode over time and can fail suddenly. If one has blown out then a replacement can simply be tapped in, but often they will start leaking and remain firmly in place.

The visco fan does a fine job when working properly but, unfortunately, often goes wrong.

To remove these a small hole can be drilled and a screw driven in so that the part can be pulled out. Another method is to tap one side, forcing the plug sideways and allowing it to be pulled out with pliers. Before driving the new plug in, the hole should be cleaned up so that the plug seals against a smooth surface. The plug must be driven in straight, otherwise it may leak.

Visco fans are notorious for either seizing, causing the fan to be engaged fully all the time – making a substantial whooshing noise and wasting fuel – or failing so that the fan never engages and the car overheats in traffic. Removing one requires a very slim spanner (specially made tools are inexpensive and save a lot of hard work) and the water pump pulley to be held stationary by clamping the belt or by holding a steadying bar such as a long square-edged screwdriver against the pulley bolt heads.

Overheating can also be caused by retarded ignition or lean running. So before taking drastic action just check the fuel and ignition settings.

Head gasket failure can cause coolant problems, depending on how

it fails. If it has failed between a coolant gallery and an oil feed, oil will be forced into the coolant, forming a film in the header tank. If it fails between the coolant gallery and an oil drain hole, coolant will get into the sump, forming a mayonnaise like emulsion in the rocker cover and a light grey sludge in the oil. If it fails between the combustion chamber and the coolant gallery, there will be clouds of white smoke, which is actually water vapour, when starting from cold, and it may blow coolant out of the pressure cap when hot. Temperature gauges are only a rough guide to engine temperature.

BRAKES

On non-ABS cars, if one wheel locks up when braking hard, check the brake on the opposite wheel as it's putting less braking force into the wheel than the side that locked up.

New rear callipers and discs ensure consistent braking in this Challenge vehicle. (Courtesy Devon 4x4)

Calliper pistons should be bright and shiny. Any flaking of the chrome finish will rip the seals when the pistons are pushed back after a pad change.

Pistons in the callipers often corrode where they're exposed to the elements between the calliper seal and the pad. Cars that have been run for long periods with worn pads will have suffered the most. Light piston corrosion can be removed with fine sandpaper, although if the chrome plating becomes damaged or begins to flake the piston and calliper seals will need replacing.

The callipers have two distinct seals on each piston. An inner seal is square in section and keeps the oil in the calliper. The square section distorts when the brakes are applied and returns the piston to its normal position when the brakes are released. If oil is leaking out then this seal has failed. The outer seal is a thinner design and its function is to keep road grime out of the calliper bore. These can become gummed up and sticky, causing the pads to constantly rub on the disc, and may result in a squealing noise when the brakes aren't on.

ABS cars will compensate for the poor performance of one calliper and prevent the other wheel locking – this hides the problem. For this reason, the callipers should be inspected yearly to check for seal and piston damage.

It's not only braking system faults that can cause a wheel to lock up when braking, worn dampers allow a wheel to bounce and reduce traction dramatically. Also, tyres have to be in good order for the braking system to apply force to the road. Incorrect tyre pressures or hardened and perished tyres reduce traction dramatically.

If the car occasionally judders at speed as if the handbrake had mysteriously come on, then there's a fair chance it has! The handbrake shoes have been known to break up into small chunks that rattle round the drum. At low speeds they just skid across the surface, but as speeds increase they eventually begin bouncing round like lottery balls and randomly jam in the mechanism. If this appears when out on an expedition, a temporary fix that some people have employed is to remove the drum, take all the pieces of broken shoe out, and refit, making a note not to use the handbrake unless absolutely necessary. However, the shoes must be replaced as soon as possible for safety.

STEERING

There are a number of parts in the steering system that can wear, and even a small amount of slack in each item can add up to a vague feeling and a tendency to wander.

Depending on model and age, the steering column will have a number of joints on its way down to the steering box; rubber couplings perish over time and even the universal joints wear. It can be checked by holding it whilst an assistant gently moves the steering wheel side to side – any loose joints need replacing.

Next in line is the steering box, which wears over time. Luckily, it has an adjustment screw so some slack can be taken up. The trouble is that the middle part of the worm gear wears the most – because we spend most of the time steering straight ahead – so if all the play is taken out when the steering is pointing straight ahead it will be too tight when at full lock. For this reason, always set the adjustment at full lock. If this results in excessive play in the straight ahead position the box will need overhaul and a new worm gear.

There are two main variations on the steering box theme, distinguished by having either three or four bolts on the top. There was also a change in mounting bolt size, from smaller imperial to larger metric bolts, so make sure you get the right ones. The mounting bolts go through the chassis and can get corroded in place, so for older vehicles it may be necessary to soak them in penetrating oil well in advance of removal. The next problem is getting the drop link off the bottom because it often seizes on to the spline.

This is a '4-bolt' steering box; the four bolts are the ones on the top plate, with the slack adjuster and lock nut in the middle.

ELECTRICS

There are two main problems with old Land Rover electrics: all the connectors age; and most cars have suffered in the hands of a keen but unskilled amateur, so have a bird's nest of added wires.

Some people 'get by' without fully understanding the system; just trying things out almost at random until the problem seems to go away. This is a potentially disastrous method. First, you don't know what the fault's root cause was, so you don't know if it has been fixed or just temporarily masked, ready to pounce later with even more venom. Secondly, you wouldn't know if you have stressed some other circuit, storing up more problems for later on. So you have to understand how the circuit works first before you can work out how to fix it.

Never make a 12-volt feed by splicing in a link to another wire nearby that had 12-volts on it, as this will increase the load on the second circuit and cause fuses to blow. Never bridge a fuse if it keeps blowing; it may be because the loom has chaffed on the bodywork and the fuse is preventing the wires burning out. The fault must be repaired first. Splicing wires together is still one of the top reasons for electrical faults on a modified car. Just twisting wires together and wrapping them in sticky tape is a recipe for disaster. Cars vibrate and go through extremes of heat and cold, and engine bays contain fuel and oil vapours, too. Not only will twisted wires loosen, but sticky tape will go soft, gooey and unwrap.

A good connection needs to start with a solid mechanical join, such as a good quality crimp. It should be strong enough that the wire cannot be tugged out. The crimp must have two elements: an inner crimp on the bare wires to make the electrical connection; and an outer crimp on the cable's insulation to

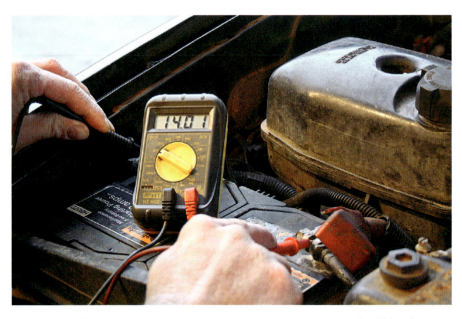

If all is well, the voltage at the battery when the engine is running should be about 14-volts. Less than 13 means the alternator is not working.

Proper crimp terminals have one crimp over the copper and one over the insulation to relieve strain on the electrical connection.

take any mechanical strain away from the conductor. Getting the right crimping force is very important: too much and the wire strands will be pinched out and break, too little and they will work loose. For this reason, it's worth investing in a ratchet crimp tool that automatically applies the right force. The alternative is to use the cheap crimp pliers and practice on scrap wire until you consistently get it right.

Soldering is another option, but as well as being a little trickier it can result in a concentration of stress at the edges of the soldered joint, leading to fractures in later life. That's why F1 cars don't use soldered joints. If you do use solder,

The crimp tool must securely fold the two wings into the wire, otherwise the connection may work loose with time.

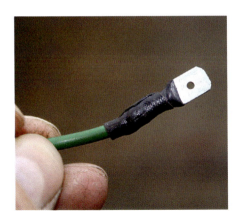

Wrapping the crimp joint in self-amalgamating tape like this, or using heat shrink tube, protects it from corrosion. Sticky insulation tape is not suitable for use in cars.

the finished joint must be wrapped with amalgamating tape or heat shrink tube in order to withstand the vibration and stresses.

Once the mechanical joint is made it must be insulated to prevent anything shorting out, and, just as importantly, to prevent moisture corroding the joint, whilst also giving the wires some strain relief. As mentioned above, a good solution is to slip a tube of 'heat shrink' plastic over the joint – when heated with a hot air gun it shrinks and seals the connection. You can even buy crimps that have integral heat shrink insulation, plus a resin that melts through the whole joint, making it very durable. Another very effective method is to use self-amalgamating rubber tape – it looks like insulating tape but isn't sticky. It's stretched and wrapped round the joint and, over a minute or so, flows into itself to form a single homogeneous, waterproof unit. It's brilliant stuff and has loads of other uses round the car, from making grommets to fixing small air leaks – every tool box should have a roll.

Sticky-backed PVC electrical insulation tape will not survive in a car for any length of time because the glue just gives up in the harsh conditions. However, PVC does have its uses. Ordinary non-sticky PVC tape, sometimes known as loom wrap, can be wound round a wiring loom to hold all the wires together neatly and protect against chafing and oxidisation. Start by threading the end of the tape into the loom and wind over it. Continue in a spiral up the loom, overlapping by about half the tape width as you go. To stop it unravelling, the final winding must be tied off by threading through the loom and tying in a knot. To finish it neatly, the ends can be dressed in self-amalgamating tape.

If the electrical fault is intermittent, try to identify what else is happening when the fault occurs: is it when something else is switched on/off, when you go over a bump, or when turning left. This will indicate where best to start looking for the fault.

Intermittent faults are frequently associated with a connector that is loose or corroded. In fact, it turns out that joints and connectors are the single most common cause of electrical problems. The pins in a connector should be bright shiny metal. If they're tarnished and very dark or if they have a white powdery surface, they must be cleaned up or replaced. Most connectors are plated in some way so scraping them will risk damaging the coating. It's best to be gentle and use spray on 'contact cleaner' and a stiff, fine-haired brush. Often, simply unplugging and reconnecting will clean the connector enough for it to work for a short time – obviously not a permanent fix but helpful in letting you know where the problem is.

Chapter 8
Modifications

"Strive for perfection in everything you do. Take the best that exists and make it better. When it doesn't exist, design it."
Henry Royce

Modified Land Rovers don't come much better equipped than this Camel Trophy Discovery built for the extremes of international competition. (Courtesy Land Rover)

Organisations like the Discovery Owners Club make owning and using a Land Rover much more rewarding.

The range of modifications possible on this chassis is quite simply amazing, from High Street luxury limousine to world-conquering competition buggy. Just thinking about the modifications possible on your own project has the power to raise a smile, and there's huge satisfaction in improving the car's capability, either on- or off-road.

This chapter summarises some of the most popular modifications that enthusiasts and professionals have tried on the huge range of Land Rover coil-sprung variants. Some work better than others, and most work best when they're done as part of an overall update of the whole car.

Just looking at the diverse range of solutions and designs at any Land Rover club meeting or off-road show brings home how many people really enjoy modifying these cars, and how much talent and imagination has gone into them.

Warning

I hope it's obvious that any modifications should only be undertaken by competent mechanics, and even though many of us have had years of experience tinkering with cars, that doesn't equate to proper qualifications.

Luckily, there is now a huge range of excellent courses available from local colleges to help enthusiasts gain these skills; from welding to electrics, it's all there and well worth the investment. If in doubt, get in a professional.

Now, most of the modifications in this chapter are intended to make the car more capable in extreme off-road conditions. This usually means that its on-road handling will be

Accidents happen, and modifications can make them either more or less likely: make sure you stay safe.

compromised and so it must be driven with due respect, and the most extreme off-roaders should not be driven on the public roads at all.

To illustrate this point, just imagine driving down a fast road and having to swerve or stop in an emergency: high centre of gravity, soft suspension, and ultra knobbly tyres all make this more tricky, and so road speeds must be reduced to compensate.

Ultimately, it's your decision on how to modify your car and how to use it, that means it's your responsibility. So stay safe.

Disclaimer

Whilst every effort has been made to ensure the information here is correct, if modifying a car ensure the information used is accurate and always follow the manufacturer's instructions.

The author doesn't recommend or advise that any of the modifications mentioned in this book should be carried out – they're presented for information only.

The author cannot accept responsibility for loss or injury as a result of modifying cars.

GENERAL TIPS

The single most important thing is that you have a very clear idea of what you want to do with the finished car.

One way to get that clear vision is to drive the standard car on the terrain you are building the car for, whether that's 'play and pay' sites, Green Lanes, or a trials section. You will learn what things you really can't live with and, equally important, which things actually work quite well already – you might be pleasantly surprised. One exception to this rule is extreme competition, where a standard car will simply fail and probably not be admitted, anyway. Instead, it's a good idea to base your modifications on the most competitive cars.

It's easy to have a dream, but successfully turning the vision into reality takes focus.

Once you know what you want to change, work out a realistic plan so you don't end up with the car stuck in the shed in an un-driveable condition for most of the year. Once you have a plan, stick to it. This is so much easier to write than to do: there will be problems on the way as things don't work out as expected, but don't fall in to the classic trap of changing the plan halfway through because that's how 'unfinished projects' are born.

Another piece of wisdom is that whatever you think might be wrong, even professional engineering companies hit unforeseen snags on new projects. So check your facts before acting on them and be prepared to learn as you go.

Stay focused on what you want to use the car for – write down your goal before you get started and keep referring back to it.

When upgrading parts, remember that making one part stronger has the potential to put more force on a neighbouring part. So always think about the forces involved and how they spread through the whole car.

Before spending a fortune on new parts, see what the standard car can do.

This competition car was built with a very clear idea of what needed to be achieved.

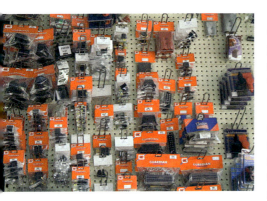

There are so many parts available for these cars that it's far too easy to get carried away and bolt on unnecessary stuff.

Making parts stronger can mean that, if they do fail, they are more likely to break than bend. This could leave the car stranded or, even worse, cause a very bad accident. As a general rule, it's better for parts to bend than snap if it all goes horribly wrong.

When bolting extra parts onto the car, make sure mounting points are suitable for the potential forces from extreme use. Check mounting points for corrosion. Many hollow sections, such as the chassis rear crossmember, can rust through from the inside, particularly if the car is taken wading through deep water. This rust might not be immediately obvious from the outside.

Weight is always worth keeping under control, many heavy-duty parts are actually very heavy. If a car is modified in stages it's easy to lose track of how much total weight has been added. A full set of protection plates, winch bumpers, and roll cage can add up to half a ton. This extra weight adversely affects handling, increases ground pressure, reduces maximum gradient and tilt angles, and increases braking distance. Increased weight means that every part of the chassis and suspension system has higher forces to cope with, and must be engineered to suit.

It's true that a car needs some weight to be good at towing and recovery work, but the Land Rover already has plenty of weight to start with.

PROTECTION

One of the most vulnerable parts of the car are the steering linkages. When crawling over rocks the first part of the car to hit is the steering drop link, and the low-hanging cross link behind the axle can get caught when the axle scrapes over obstacles – resulting in a bent bar and massive toe out.

The steering links are quite vulnerable. Here, an uprated link has been fitted, as well as moving the steering damper higher up.

For this reason, there are a great number of heavy-duty bars available which are much more rigid. Some bars have a separate outer tube running their whole length, which can freely rotate on the inner shaft so that as it contacts obstacles it rolls rather than drags.

But if the bar doesn't bend it can put more force on the ball joints. Imagine driving over a rock which raises the whole car up on the bar. If the bar bends you realise something is wrong and stop to bend it back, but if the bar stays rigid the whole car is raised up on the ball joints, which could break and leave the car stranded. So it's not as clear a choice as it may first seem.

Another way of saving the steering

A good bolt-on steering guard can also provide sturdy recovery points.

links is to fit a protection plate. A front-mounted steering guard will save the drag link from most dangers on a Green Lane, but still leaves some vulnerability at extreme axle angles. These are available as one-piece or three-piece assemblies. The three-piece has separate side plates that bolt to the chassis, but, as the main protection plate is held on to the side plates with bolts, it can be slightly weaker than a one-piece. A one-piece unit has to be made accurately to line up with the chassis, although it can be more difficult to fit because chassis dimensions can vary.

The guard is a substantial piece of equipment so it's worth thinking about incorporating recovery points into it, too.

The steering cross link behind the front axle can be protected by bolting a C-section protector plate onto the differential housing, preventing it from being bent back.

The front differential is very vulnerable: it's made of steel sheet that is a little thinner than would be ideal, and it's the lowest part of the axle. Diff protection covers come in many varieties. Some are bolt-on units, and the simplest is a plate that bolts to the underside of the main diff casing, extending forwards and up over the

The steering link behind the axle is low and vulnerable. This substantial guard bolts on to the diff housing.

In the old days, some people used the ends of gas cylinders to make weld-on diff protectors, but now we have superb custom-made units for the job. (Courtesy Devon 4x4)

lower edge of the diff pan. These are very good for sliding over obstacles as long as there's no danger of the obstacle hitting the exposed part of the pan. Because of their size, these units they can be quite heavy and trap mud and stones.

Another variant is a thicker pan cover that uses a large band clamp to hold on to the perimeter of the diff pan. However, whilst this is simple to fit, it can work loose and fall off, particularly when reversing over rocks. Another potential problem is the clamp knocking paint off of the diff pan, which can

promote rust. The guard can also fill up with mud, making the corrosion problem worse. But for occasional work, being fitted only when needed, these can be a useful addition.

A much more resilient option is a weld on guard; similar to the bolt-on unit but welded-on to the diff pan. The same problem of filling with mud exists, though, so they can be bad for corrosion.

A better solution is to fit a completely new diff pan made from much thicker material. This requires cutting the old pan out, and the axle has to be removed and stripped to avoid damage to the differential.

Re-engineering the axle with a strong steel support plate and a bolt-on high strength alloy cast pan is the ultimate protection.

The rear axle is less vulnerable than the front as it faces in the opposite direction and the soft diff pan is only at risk when reversing or dropping off rocks. The parts that fit the front axle can also fit the rear one, but there are simpler options in the form of a plate bolted to the diff case underside. This extends backwards, and can also have a kick up at the front to protect the input shaft.

Side steps can offer a little sill protection, but usually they're attached via fairly weak plates onto the side of the chassis body mounts, which will buckle if heavily loaded. They also reduce ground clearance a little, too.

Defender jackable sills benefit from bolting directly to the substantial chassis outriggers.

Rock sliders/jackable sills, on the other hand, are designed to do exactly what the name suggests, and can be slid along big rocks or be used to jack the whole car up. One of the problems with this on Range Rover and Discovery models is that the body is held onto the chassis with relatively lightweight rubber mountings, so jacking the car up on the body would put these mounts under a lot of stress.

One solution is to mount the rock sliders just outside the existing sills and effectively replace the sill trim piece. The slider then bolts to the chassis via substantial brackets.

Another solution is to replace the existing sills with the rock sliders and reinforce the body mounts, removing the noise isolating rubbers and fitting solid spacers. However, this still places strain on the mounting brackets that they weren't designed for so extra reinforcing stays may be required. Defenders are simpler as the body is solidly mounted to more substantial outriggers.

Race cars with the engine positioned further back in the chassis have a sump guard integrated into a new centre crossmember, usually guarding

For serious bash protection this competition car has extra tubing welded-on to protect the sill.

A gearbox guard being fabricated onto a new bolt-in crossmember.
(Courtesy Devon 4x4)

bend them. Stronger ones are available, which are capable of being dragged over rocks without deformation.

The rear trailing arms are just steel rod and a little more prone to bending on very rocky crawls; again, replacement heavy-duty parts can be bolted in place.

The fuel tank is behind the rear axle and is reasonably out of the way. Early models were fitted with a steel tank that can rust and become weak; the later plastic tank is a lot more resilient. As standard there's a thin protection plate that runs the length of the tank, but doesn't quite go all the way to the edges. This is fine for most purposes, but if reversing in rocky terrain there's a risk of damage, so protection plates that bolt-on to the standard plate mounting points are available.

This heavy-duty tank guard covers the full width of the tank, and also incorporates mounting points for a towing bracket or recovery point.

CAGES

Roll cages stop the cab collapsing if the car rolls, and designs depend on what sort of use the car will get. Comp Safari racers tend to go for an internal cage where the main hoop bolts through the body onto the chassis. It has two rear stays extending into the load bed to which the front cage is attached, following the roof edge and extending down the A-pillar to the floor. This keeps the outside of the car smooth,

An external roll cage protects the bodywork. (Courtesy Devon 4x4)

The front tubes go through the wing and bolt securely to the chassis.
(Courtesy Devon 4x4)

minimising the chances of it becoming snagged on bits of scenery. It's also the lightest competition cage layout.

Challenge vehicles tend to have the cage mounted outside the bodywork. Rolling is more likely on these events, but it will be at a low speed and the cage can protect the bodywork, as well as providing plenty of options for attaching recovery gear. An external cage doesn't take up any room inside the cabin, which is already in short supply on a Defender.

For a Play Day car a simpler cage is available. A main hoop attaches through the body to the middle of the chassis and to two back stays. Without the back

both engine and gearbox sumps. When the engine is moved back eight inches or so, the standard crossmember fouls the engine, so the new item has to be a lot smaller in height. To make up for the loss in rigidity, the lower part can be stiffened with a 3mm wall half-inch box section and a further crosspiece attached using the original gearbox mounting holes a few inches behind the main crossmember. A skid plate is attached which is raised at the front so as to act a bit like a ski when everything bottoms out.

The front radius arms are fairly strong, but if rock crawling there's a risk that the car could drop onto them and

The Defender SVX had a cage as standard; without rear diagonals and with the front bars mounted to the wing. It was not intended for competition use but adds purpose to a road car. (Courtesy Land Rover)

Top: This is why competition vehicles need cages! (Courtesy Devon 4x4)

Above: An internal cage partly installed; the lower feet bolt directly to substantial mountings welded onto the main chassis members. (Courtesy Devon 4x4)

stays the main hoop could be levered backwards in a roll to leave the cab exposed.

Cages need to be attached to the chassis rather than body: the body is weakly mounted to the chassis and doesn't have enough strength on its own.

Internal roll cages can be dangerous in an accident where it's possible for occupants to hit their heads against the hard steel tube. For this reason, an internal cage should only be used in conjunction with competition seats and harnesses to hold the occupants steady, and also with crash helmets to protect the skull.

Aluminium 'show' cages offer no protection and in an accident the tubes can crease up and form potentially lethal razor sharp edges. They have no place on real cars.

BULL BARS

Front protection bars, known as bull bars, brush bars, roo bars, and even nerf or nudge bars are probably the most contentious piece of equipment that can be fitted to a car. In many countries they're banned outright so if you are planning an international

A traditional frontal protection bar: it has many names and is generally hated by people who know very little about it.

trip it's worth checking first. At time of writing, the law in the UK requires all bars made after 2005 to be tested for pedestrian safety (2005/66/EC). This is why the official Land Rover items now come with rubberised padding and will collapse if hit hard, which makes their usefulness as a protection system a bit questionable.

The main use of such bars is to reduce damage to the front of the car when driving past overgrown trees or bushes, and to protect the corners when manoeuvring in tight off-road situations. Additionally, some bars extend under the front of the car to provide steering protection, too. It's quite common for the bars to be used to mount extra lighting, and to have extra protection for the headlight and indicator areas.

In other countries, such as Australia, bars can provide protection from the larger wild animals that sometimes leap into the path of oncoming cars, and so have a slightly different design. In some countries where risk of damage is very high, bull bars are considered essential safety equipment. However, because they're heavy and can pose increased risk to pedestrians, it's best to avoid bull bars unless you really need them.

A useful, heavy-duty bumper incorporating a winch, jacking points, and provision for extra lights.

Brush wires are surprisingly useful for preventing small branches from hitting the windscreen, especially if competing in a jungle! (Courtesy Land Rover)

So a very valuable thing to do is drive your intended course in the standard car first; see where it's lacking and where it already works very well. Land Rovers are actually very good off-road as standard – that's what they were designed for!

Land Rovers are usually modified to increase articulation – how far the wheels can move up and down – and ground clearance – the gap between the underside of the car and the ground. On very rough ground the standard car can end up with one or two wheels in the air, either because the suspension can't move far enough or because the car has ground out on its belly and a wheel in the air obviously has no traction. When this happens the standard differentials conspire against you by allowing the free wheel to spin, and so no drive goes to the other wheel that is still on the ground. This is where a locking or limited slip differential comes in handy, ensuring at least some drive goes to the wheel with traction. This relieves some of the burden on the suspension when on dry ground, but on slippery surfaces you need all the tyre contact area you can get.

Big travel suspension systems using longer springs can help maintain

An equally useful heavy-duty rear bumper; made to look like the original item but produced from thick steel and incorporating recovery and jacking points.

Brush wires run from the top corners of the windscreen to either the front wing edges or the bull bar. They prevent overhanging brush and small branches from hitting the screen, and can be very handy on Green Lanes, particularly in the spring before any lane maintenance has been done. They need to be fairly tight and have secure mounting points. Note: never drill into the A-pillar to mount equipment as this will compromise the car's strength.

SUSPENSION

Talk to any ten enthusiasts about Land Rover suspension and you will get ten different opinions of what works and what is just plain rubbish; it's one of those areas where there seems to be a lot more opinion than fact.

Unfortunately, there are many bull bars on the market that are built for looks and perform very badly when used in anger: some are made from thin walled tube which crumples too easily and affords no real protection; some have minimal mounting points that fail when loaded.

A good bar system should not reduce the beam of the headlights or obscure the indicators, and should allow easy cleaning of the light lens and bulb replacement.

A standard Land Rover is actually very capable already. The best cars only have modifications where they need them. (Courtesy Land Rover)

Huge articulation keeps the tyres on the ground; this trials machine uses it to the full. (Courtesy Devon 4x4)

As a car is lifted, the front axle tilts forward and changes the castor angle.

Rear suspension stability is heavily influenced by the A-arm, and quality bushes are definitely needed. (Courtesy Devon 4x4)

Longer springs can allow the axle to move further, and also hold the body higher to avoid obstacles.

the tyre's contact patch on very uneven tracks, but there's a trade off here. The car is raised, making it less stable on corners, and off-road this means side slopes become much more of a problem – and having a car that falls over on its side on a course where little Suzuki's just drive past is damn embarrassing, not to mention potentially dangerous. More importantly, on-road emergency manoeuvres can become significantly less safe, and this is made worse by big soft tyres.

A 2in lift is very popular and 4in is considered rather high, but suits big tyres. Changing ride height will change the front castor angle: going higher reduces it, making the steering lighter but less stable at speed: dropping it increases castor, making the steering heavier and the car reluctant to go round corners. One way of fixing this is with off-set front radius arm bushes. These allow up to 2.5 degrees of correction, but they can, in extreme circumstances, drift out of position so a better, but more expensive, solution is special castor corrected radius arms.

The rear axle has a huge influence on steering stability and any wear in the top A-arm bushes, ball joint, or links will result in a vague feeling when you turn the wheel. Although polyurethane bushes will tighten things up, a good set of standard rubber bushes are actually not bad and will freshen up a tired car. Cheap polyurethane bush sets may be poor quality and can fall apart, so fit good ones, such as SuperPro or Polybush. For serious rear axle stability you can break out the welding kit and adapt the axle casing and chassis to accept front axle 'hockey sticks' which also increase roll resistance quite dramatically. This is a big job and the Panhard rod that is needed to control side movement will require mods to the fuel tank for clearance. It's such a good mod that it was adopted as standard on the Discovery 2. Indeed, a set of Discovery 2 axles make a very nice conversion, but they're not cheap and will require significant chassis mods, and also matching wheels due to the smaller pitch circle diameter (PCD).

Later Range Rovers and Discoveries after '94 had anti-roll bars that made a big difference to stability, particularly if you have a heavy load.

Front hockey sticks on the rear axle of the author's Range Rover-based Tomcat add hugely to high speed stability.

Polyurethane bushes are firmer than rubber and last longer, adding stability and durability.

Prepare the suspension for fitting the bushes by removing any sharp burrs and coating with soapy water.

These can be retrofitted, but do require a simple bracket to be welded onto the chassis. The front and rear bars have to be a matching set because it will affect the way a car handles in an emergency quite a lot: stiffer rear bars increase

Most bushes are fitted easily by hand, but some of the tighter ones need a vice with protective plates to spread the force evenly over the bush.

This Discovery has anti-roll bars but extreme suspension travel is hardly limited at all ...

oversteer; stiffer front bars increase understeer – oversteer is considered to be more dangerous than understeer. You can also get uprated bars that increase roll resistance even more, and are useful for taming lifted cars.

The ball joints and steering drag links are relatively weak, and tougher ones are available which will reduce the chances of getting stranded. Bigger tyres and a heavier car put more strain on these, but they're not very expensive so should be budgeted for in any big project.

As well as longer springs, there are some other tricks to consider. One popular mod is to allow the springs to dislocate from their seats so the weight of the axle and wheel makes it drop to the ground. The only weight pushing the tyre into the ground is half the axle and a wheel, so there's significantly less traction available than from the other wheel on the same axle, and, again, some form of slip limiting in the diff can help – or just drive gently so as to not ask too much from it. When the wheel comes back up there needs to be some sort of relocation device to make the spring sit back in the right place, usually in the form of steel cones or spikes.

... compared to this Range Rover without anti-roll bars, which manages to get very slightly further, though the difference is small.

Ball joints and link bars have to transmit large forces; uprated ones are a useful improvement.

The relocation cone in the spring seat allows the spring to drop freely on very rough ground and still return to its seat. (Courtesy Devon 4x4)

The damper top mount here has a swivel joint to allow extra movement. (Courtesy Devon 4x4)

Another thing that limits wheel drop is the suspension linkages, and in particular the bushes, which can only bend so far before binding up and restricting movement. One way round this is to replace the bushed links with links that have a spherical-type joint in them, and mount to dedicated mounting plates. Monster articulation will also require modified propshafts to cope with the extreme angles.

ROAD BIAS

Of course, not every Land Rover is modified for ultimate off-road capability; many spend most of their lives on the road, often towing large trailers. The on-road handling can be improved without totally ruining the off-road ability: it wont be spectacular off-road, but it wont be exactly bad either.

The methods are almost the complete opposite of the ones mentioned above. The first step is the tyres, and good road tyres cost money – see the tyres section for more info.

After that, look to reduce unnecessary play in the suspension system. A good starting point is the bushes. Replacing old rubber bushes with good quality new rubber makes a big difference. After all, these cars didn't handle too badly when they were new, and restoring them to that condition really is a good first step. To go further, you could consider polyurethane bushes, which are available in a variety of firmnesses – stiffer bushes make tauter handling but transmit a little more noise.

The next thing to tackle is roll; to improve handling and make the car feel nicer to drive round twisty roads. Generally, stiffer springs are not such a good move,

Keeping the suspension low, using anti-roll bars and stiff bushes makes a road biased car more responsive, and aids towing stability.

The steering damper makes the car more stable at speed; this one is mounted high on the front steering link for protection.

they can make the ride a bit too harsh and, whilst they will reduce roll, they can make the axle skitter over rough back road surfaces. It's far better to use firmer dampers with standard springs. Colin Chapman, founder of Lotus Cars, famously defined perfect suspension as soft springs firmly damped.

Anti-roll bars add a useful amount of stability, especially on raised vehicles, and can be retrofitted to most older Land Rovers.

Although dropping the ride height will compromise its spectacular off-road ability, it will still be fine if you are only going to climb kerbs and pull a trailer out of a muddy field. Indeed, the original car was dropped nearly an inch to reduce roll in about '83. Dropping it a further inch will noticeably improve its road manners, but you will need to trim half the depth off the bump stops, too.

WHEELS AND TYRES

The most important component on any car is the tyres – no really, it is. Tyres are the only component linking the car to the ground so choosing the right ones makes all the difference. But when all is said and done, tyres are a personal choice. Often there will be a selection of possible tyres that will all do what you want, but one model will seem to fit the image you have in your head better than the others. Although, if you buy tyres based just on which looks best, don't be too surprised if they don't work quite as well as you had hoped!

This Simex tyre shows battle scars from serious competition. It has a close tread pattern in the centre and a wide set of big lugs at the side, as well as tread on the sidewall, covering most eventualities.

Road use

For mainly road use there are very good performance tyres, such as the Pirelli Scorpion S/T or Yoko Geolandar AT, which make a huge difference to handling, and are still absolutely fine for Green Laning and exceptionally useful on snow and ice-covered winter roads.

Chunky off-road tyres can be very vague on road and lead to snaking under braking – best avoided if your

The Pirelli Scorpion S/T provides good grip on snow and ice, as well as excellent road performance.

Ultra low profile tyres don't work so well with these cars due to lack of compliance.

main use is on road or towing a heavy trailer.

There are different tyres for summer and winter use, and in many countries swapping to winter tyres when the cold weather starts is compulsory. Winter

The right tyres not only dictate the car's performance but are an essential part of its image. (Courtesy Devon 4x4)

tyres have a softer compound and lots of small deep blocks with extra tiny groves in so they can even get some grip on ice.

Winter tyres don't work so well in summer: at speed the narrow tread blocks wobble about and overheat which loses grip. So it's worth having separate sets for winter and summer.

Low profile tyres on big wheels don't work well on these cars. They cause the axles to be jolted about on the more uneven back roads, which makes the steering feel nervous and twitchy. Off-road they're less flexible and don't offer the same traction as a higher profile tyre. Standard profile tyres offer a far more relaxed drive.

Off-road use

This is where it gets tricky. Each type of terrain requires a different type of tyre, so you often end up having to compromise in one way or another.

For muddy tracks there are two scenarios. The first is where there's a few inches of mud, with gravel or rock underneath. It may be best to use narrow tyres here that will sink through the mud and get a good grip on the solid ground underneath. The other scenario is where there's no solid ground underneath, at least not within the reach of the tyres anyway. Here you need a wide tyre that will 'float' on top of the mud with big lugs to dig in and give traction. Consideration must be given to the area you are driving through, if it's a Green Lane then you should not be doing any damage to the track so

The choice of tyre is bewildering, but each design is tailored to a specific use.

having a tyre that cuts the ground up is a definite no no.

The tyre carcass makes a big difference, too. A softer one allows the tread area to flex over the lumps and bumps on the ground, giving more traction, but it's also more susceptible to punctures and on long expeditions the drop in fuel economy can be a problem.

One of the problems with mud is that it sticks in between the tread blocks and effectively renders the tread smooth. Tyres designed for mud have deep channels radiating out from the centre of the tread in a chevron pattern, so that as the tyre moves forwards the mud is pushed out sideways. But on sand, a mud tyre would simply cut down too deep, so a close tread pattern, similar to road tyres, is much better. Gravel tyres are designed with channels about the width of the gravel pieces, so they're gripped between the small flexible tread blocks. On mud these would just clog instantly, and even wet grass can send them sliding.

Some tyres have a mixture of tread types with a denser central band of

A narrower tyre can outperform a wide tyre where it has to sink through surface mud to reach hard ground. (Courtesy Land Rover)

This tyre has become blocked with sticky yet slippery mud, resulting in the winch being needed. (Courtesy Devon 4x4)

The tyre carcass has a substantial influence on performance; softer ones can have better grip at the expense of resistance to damage and punctures.

The chevron tread pattern has forced the sticky mud out into a band at the side of the tyre.

Of course, you could start making your own monster truck. Here, the tyre is offered up to work out wheelarch modifications. (Courtesy Devon 4x4)

blocks for road and sand but getting wider spacing towards the tyre edge to cope with softer ground. Many 4x4 tyres have lugs that extend past the sidewall, so if the tyre does sink these more aggressive chunks will get a grip.

Very deep tread blocks and softer rubber on the most aggressive off-road tyres makes the tread unstable on-road, leading to reduced braking performance and lower grip when cornering, as well as increased wear and a loud droning noise at speed. Broader tread blocks are more stable and last longer, but would slide on gravel. So with all these different aspects of tyre design there isn't one universally good tyre, if the car is to be used in a range of terrains then it may be worth having a spare set of wheels with different tyres on. For example, mud tyres for Play Days and road biased tyres for every day use.

Under pressure

Tyre pressures are critical, and the book values may not always be best if you have non-standard tyres: up to 40psi may be needed on-road, depending on usage, and dropping the pressures significantly can aid traction on very soft surfaces off-road.

On an older car where annual mileages are limited, the tread will often outlast the casing. Six years should be considered too old for any tyre, no matter what it looks like on the outside; just because it still holds air doesn't necessarily mean it's in good condition. Those little hairline cracks can run very deep and you never know when one will develop into a complete puncture. Tyres can stay up on project cars for many decades, but a perished tyre can blow out suddenly when the car is taken up to speed, or when cornering, so it's a dangerous game of roulette – not to be played on public roads.

Tyre markings

Taking a 235/80R16 99S tyre as an example:
'235': section width of the tyre carcass in mm. Usually slightly wider than the tread, to the nearest 5mm.
'80': the side-walls measure 80 per cent of the section width.
'R': radial layout of the cords.
'16': wheel diameter in inches.
'99': static (car parked) load index, this one is 775kg.
'S': the actual maximum speed rating, 113mph here. Older tyres had this rating where the 'Z' is instead.

Since 2000, tyre markings also include a date code, such as '3508' (made in the 35th week of '08). As mentioned above, tyres over 6 years should never be used.

The pressure rating is a maximum and not the pressure you should run at.

Traction, temperature, performance, and wear rates are also given a relative code, but actual performance depends on use.

The alternative notation has this in inches instead, a 750/16 has a width of 7.5in on a 16in wheel. Yet another variation might be 37x12.5R16, which means a 37in total diameter and 12.5in width.

Wheels

Don't think that for hard off-road use you will necessarily need to buy new wheels. For instance, the standard Vogue alloys are very strong and quite light. These get overlooked by many so are quite cheap.

There are some differences between similar looking wheels on different models. Most importantly,

Standard alloys are surprisingly tough, and can be made to look smart, too.

Steel wheels have the advantage that dents can usually be knocked out; they bend rather than break.

the standard steel wheels fitted to Defenders were wider metal than the almost identical ones fitted to Discoveries – to cope with the Defender's higher possible gross vehicle weight, combined with the perception that Defenders will be used in much harder terrain – the upshot being if you want to save weight on a Defender race car you could use Discovery wheels, and if you are using a Discovery in heavy rock-strewn terrain then you could use Defender wheels.

Discovery 2 and P38 Range Rover models use a smaller BMW PCD. An adaptor kit will allow you to tap into a vast range of cheap alloy wheels,

Competition steel wheels with a bolt-on bead lock ring and a protective hoop over the valve.

but its cost makes it a questionable conversion.

Land Rover offered wheels up to 18in for these cars, but there are a huge variety of aftermarket wheels up to a quite remarkable 24in. Beware of uncertified cheap wheels. Unfortunately, there are no legal test requirements in the UK for wheels, and there have been stories of badly made wheels breaking up at high speed or in high-load situations. Any quality wheel will have the manufacturers mark and the date when it was made either stamped or cast in. If a wheel has no markings ask yourself this; why would any proud manufacturer not put their name to their product, what are they trying to hide? The mark is usually in the hub area or on the inside of one of the spokes.

There are some voluntary tests manufacturers can put their wheels through. For example, there's a Japanese test that all Original Equipment Manufacturer (OEM) wheels go through. The resulting mark looks a bit like 'JWL' but is in fact a Japanese character – this is a good sign to have on any wheel.

The other markings it should have are the size and rim style. Taking 7j17 as an example: '7' means that the wheel is 7in wide between the tyre bead seats; 'j' refers to the shape of the bead seat; and '17' indicates a 17in diameter at the bead seat. All these dimensions must match the tyre's requirements, including the letter.

There's more to nut design than meets the eye. Steel wheels usually use nuts or bolts with a tapered shoulder, so that they naturally tend to centralise in the hole. Most, but not all, alloy wheels use sleeve nuts or bolts that have flat shoulders and a cylindrical part that fits inside the hole. The two are not interchangeable – both put force into the wheel at very different angles – and using the wrong ones may crack the wheel. Make sure you get the right nuts for your new wheels.

Wheels are available with a variety of offsets to suit different applications.

Obviously, the wheel has to sit centrally on the hub, otherwise it would mean a very bumpy ride. There are two main ways that car manufacturers do this: one is to use the hub centre to locate the middle of the wheel, known as 'Hub Centric'; the other is to use the nuts to do the job, known as 'Bolt Centric.' Although all Land Rover models have used the same wheel

PCD since 1948, the hub centres have changed very slightly. Older cars were never offered with an alloy option, and had a very slightly bigger hub centre for the steel wheels, using Bolt Centric location. However, approximately coincident with the launch of the Vogue models, Land Rovers used Hub Centric location instead because it's the best method for alloy wheels, allowing them to take higher forces in off-road conditions. The hole in the middle of the wheel has to be precisely machined to fit over the hub centre in order to achieve this, though. Unfortunately, because many aftermarket wheels have general purpose centres, you will have to fit a plastic spacer to make it fit your car properly, and in off-road use these spacers can get mashed. It's safest to use wheels designed to fit the Land Rover without the need for spacers.

The difference is only about a millimetre, but it does mean that early axles won't take later steel wheels or alloys without modification. To get round this, cut a small amount of metal out of the wheels on a lathe, or, more sensibly, fit the later type of hub to the axles.

Wheels can be designed to position the tyres more inboard or outboard of the car. Tyres are outset if they stick out a long way, and inset if they're tucked well inside the wheelarch. Offset is the term used to describe the position of the wheels – how outset or inset they are on a car – and it has a big effect on handling. Having wheels poking out of the arches may look good, and in the past people have used standard wheels fitted with thick spacers on the hub to achieve this, but it completely changes the way the tyre pulls on the suspension. It's the same with wheels made with a high outset, such as 'deep dish' alloys. Imagine hitting a pothole or rock with the left front tyre, if it's sticking out a long way from the car then the force pushing the tyre backwards, caused by the impact, makes the wheel turn left. In bad cases this can rip the steering wheel out of the driver's hand and cause the car to swerve off the road.

Even changing the offset by a few millimetres makes a difference to how the steering fights back, so it's crucial to get wheels with the right offset.

At 'full bump' the tyre tucks deep into the arch; even a slightly bigger tyre would touch the back of the arch and the upper lip. (Courtesy James Ferguson)

Bolt-on arch kits are simple to fit and look purposeful. (Courtesy Devon 4x4)

Fitting bigger tyres means that they're closer to the cars bodywork and suspension parts. The first problem most people encounter is at the front axle where the wide tyre hits the front radius arm when turning tight corners. Big aggressive tyres with large tread lugs can even jam against the arm and lock the wheel up. it's important to wind the lock stop adjustment bolt on the axle out so that the tyre cannot foul the radius arm. Obviously, this reduces the manoeuvrability and increases the turning radius, so you have to weigh up the advantages of big tyres against the loss of cornering ability.

The next problem is when the wheel is pushed up and hits the wheelarch. If it's only just touching the arch metalwork it may be possible to roll the edge of the wheelarch flat, giving a little more clearance, but for big clashes the metal must be cut away. Road cars must have arches that cover the full width of the tyres when in the straight ahead position. This means wide tyres may require arch extenders or spats, and where metal is cut away there must be no sharp edges, so some form of finishing is needed anyway.

The Defender rubber or plastic flexible arch trims can be made to fit both Discovery and Range Rover arches with a bit of hard work and some cutting, but aftermarket arch kits made for the job are also available. For off-road use only, some people use cheap wheelarches from trailer suppliers, cut in half and riveted on – it might not look very sophisticated but it works very well.

Alternative spare wheel mounting

There are three very important things to bear in mind here: wheels are heavy

A swing-away wheel carrier takes the stress off the door.

so the location must be strong enough to take the forces when bumping over rocks etc; safety must be maintained so the spare shouldn't obscure visibility or add weight too high up; you have to be able to get it off in an emergency.

It can be tempting to mount it on the bonnet, just like some of the older Series Land Rovers, but there are problems with this. A heavy wheel and tyre will make it difficult to open the bonnet: it could be an extra 40kg, more for steel wheels with big tyres, and it's a lot to lift when your hands are slippery with mud. Also, most bonnets can't take the added weight safely without modification – consider what happens as the vehicle is being forced about in the off-road conditions you intend to put it through – but an even more testing requirement is that it doesn't come off in a road crash where forces can exceed 20g easily: meaning that 40kg wheel just became nearly a ton of force trying to rip itself out of the bonnet and become a missile.

So, obviously, the wheel mounting

Standard solid discs are quite up to most jobs if in good condition.
(Courtesy Devon 4x4)

Vented discs reduce fade when used heavily; the cooling air is drawn from the centre.
(Courtesy Devon 4x4)

Bonnet mounts have to be reinforced to spread the load into the bonnet, and they also make the bonnet heavy to open.

Range Rover callipers on the left, and later Defender 110 items on the right.

has to be sturdy and spread the load over a reasonably large amount of the bonnet. A common method is to use either the Discovery or Defender spare wheel mounting bracket with a large load-spreading plate under the bonnet. This puts the force through the bonnet, so the hinges and latch need to be up to the job, too.

It's pretty much the same story for body side mounting and roof mounting; both requiring appropriate strengthening. Bear in mind that roof mounting will add more weight higher up and increase the car's tendency to roll – plus lifting that much weight that high can be hard work!

Defender standard rear door wheel mounts can distort the door when a heavier tyre is fitted. Swing-away carriers use a hinged steel tube frame to mount the wheel that bolts to the door frame instead, which is much stronger.

BRAKES

Before uprating the brakes, consider what you are trying to achieve. All-round solid discs are fine for most purposes

and for off-road competition; after all, you can't brake overly hard on mud, and vented discs just fill up with mud which defeats their purpose. But for towing, the vented front discs fitted to later models offer far better fade resistance. The front callipers are the AP four pots used on the SD1, Princess, and many other cars of the '70s, so upgrade parts are available. Moving to harder pads will improve braking, such as 'Green Stuff' from EBC, and many uprated discs are available, but avoid crack-prone crossdrilled types. Some later Defender 110s used bigger four pot callipers and different vented discs for a further bolt-on and cheap improvement for other models. There are more

Full-on high speed race brakes, with a separate bolt-on centre 'bell' fitted to a Bowler Wildcat.
(Courtesy Bowler Off-road)

extreme conversions using Brembo and Alcon parts costing a few thousand pounds, but these need very good traction to be fully effective so good suspension and tyres is a must, too. These are best suited to road biased cars; excellent for heavy towing etc.

A word of warning: very powerful brakes on off-road biased cars can break traction, particularly on knobbly tyres, making it more difficult to control in an emergency.

The brake bias needs to be carefully considered, too. If you have a raised car, braking heavily will pitch it forwards more than a standard car. This takes downforce away from the rear wheels and can make them lock-up more easily. Cars with ABS get round this problem to a large extent, but are not totally immune. Those without ABS need the brake bias adjusting forwards to compensate. This isn't a job for the amateur, so seek advice from professionals when considering your own particular project.

Remember that if the suspension travel is increased the brake hoses must be longer, too, and because they will be more exposed they should be carefully routed to minimise the chance of them being snagged. Some racers run the front flexible hoses along the radius arms and protect them with a shield so the only exposed parts are the short lengths at the body mount and the wheel hub.

ENGINES

Land Rover traditionally used very low-power engines, designed to be ultra-reliable in harsh environments and able to run on the poor quality fuels often found in remote parts of the world. Originally, it was also felt that high power would upset long travel off-road suspension. This is why the 3.5-litre V8 in Defender models was

The Rover V8 is beautifully simple and fairly lightweight.

tuned down to only 111bhp, when the same engine in the Rover SD1 saloon car was rated at up to 190bhp.

Since the early days of the Range Rover, attitudes have changed and technology has moved on. The current top of the range Land Rovers produce over 500bhp, and applying some of this knowledge to older cars can not only improve performance, making towing easier, but can also improve economy.

DIESEL ENGINE TUNING

The Land Rover 200Tdi unit is a solid and reliable 2.5-litre turbo that can be tweaked to about 130bhp on a modest

budget with mods to the pump and a bigger intercooler. The 300Tdi is a redesigned 200Tdi, and offers easier servicing and a little more tuning potential. A popular and simple mod is to unscrew the top of the boost capsule, turn it 180°, and refit it, which instantly improves pedal response and makes the car feel quite nippy. More expensive mods include head work, mechanical pump mods, and a bigger intercooler, which can produce performance similar to that of the 3.5-litre V8 petrol but with over 30mpg potential.

The TD5 unit from a Discovery 2 or Defender adds real performance – the potential for over 200bhp and torque of over 300lb/ft – with a new tune in the ECU and a bigger intercooler. New technology variable geometry turbos can be fitted to help spread the torque band out and, combined with intercooler and tune mods, produce over 230bhp.

Tuning the other diesels in the

The 200 and 300 Tdi engines can be modestly tuned, and give strong reliable power if well-maintained.

The simplest tuning modification on the 300Tdi is to unbolt the boost capsule top, rotate it 180 degrees, and refit it.

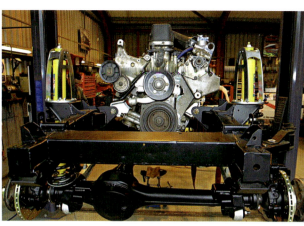

A well-tuned Rover V8 can produce over 300bhp, but anything over 200bhp starts getting expensive. (Courtesy Devon 4x4)

range, such as the TD or VM, will return fairly small gains and it may be much more cost effective to change the engine for one of the later units.

Diesel LPG

The idea is that a relatively small amount of LPG is introduced into an otherwise un-modified diesel engine to increase the flame speed in the combustion chamber, resulting in more of the diesel being converted into useful power and effectively improving the efficiency. This is claimed to improve fuel economy by up to 25 per cent, as well as increase performance massively by up to 80 per cent, particularly on turbo engines where the turbo lag is almost completely eliminated. Obviously, this extra power puts additional strain on the engine, as with any tuning method, so long-term durability will be affected, although this does depend on how hard the engine is used and may be offset by improved maintenance.

If the system is fitted as a DIY kit then it's vital to get it set up by a professional. The performance gains are quite remarkable and there's a huge temptation to put more and more

LPG in, but it's very easy to overdo it and melt the engine. The amount of gas admitted depends on engine speed and load, so good systems use a small electronic control box to control a gas solenoid or injector based on signals from the tacho and accelerator pedal position. The unit also provides some safety features ensuring gas cannot be injected into a stalled engine.

Done properly this is a wonderful tuning method, giving much greater gains than conventional diesel tuning methods with the added bonus of better fuel economy, and can give many years of reliable service. But done badly it will be short-lived and very costly.

ENGINE TUNING
Rover V8

For years the only option was the venerable Rover V8, which is still a very good engine with reasonable power from the lightweight unit. Tuning up to 300bhp with the later 4.6-litre block is achievable on a reasonable budget, but anything above this requires disproportionate investment.

The basic 3.5-litre engine in 110 carb guise produced only 114bhp, but using a standard LR 4.2-litre cam retarded 3 degrees, high compression pistons, a decent sports air filter, proper mapping, and decent exhaust headers can yield in the region of 200bhp. The standard 3.9-litre gave 185bhp, and the rare 4.2-litre 210bhp, offering a relatively simple engine swap upgrade. The early Bosch/Lucas L-Jetronic air meter 'flapper' is a little restrictive. The later 14CUX control system is a much better and very tunable, and some people use the larger air flow meter off

a six-cylinder Jag for a bit more flow. If you swap to the later 4.0- or 4.6-litre block you will need to make some mods. The crank nose is different where it drives a concentric oil pump, the cam no longer drives the oil pump, and most do not have a distributor. So if you want to use a distributor you'll need the very rare 'intermediate' front cover, although you are better off using your own ECU, such as an Emerald, and ditching the distributor anyway. A 4.6-litre with a hot cam, a bit of head work, a free flow exhaust, and a decent air filter can give 300bhp reliably.

Janspeed made a turbo kit many years ago and a few companies have made supercharger conversions. Sometimes these come up secondhand and can be tempting, but they will need setting up properly, and beware of broken unobtainable parts.

4-pot petrol engine

The old Land Rover four-cylinder engine was standard fit in Defenders in their early days. It's a very old design and, although very reliable – making it a real contender for expedition vehicles – it has very limited tuning potential. So if more performance is required, swapping it for a later engine may be a better idea.

2.0 Mpi

The Rover 4 pot was fitted in Discoveries for a few years, mainly for tax reasons, and struggles to pull the two tonne car. Although there's a plethora of tuning mods for the standard engine, perhaps the easiest way to achieve significant gains is to swap in the Rover Turbo version with performance to match a standard V8.

Engine swap

One way of getting more performance is to fit a completely different engine, and the simplest approach is to use another Land Rover unit. Looking through the Land Rover parts catalogue shows how they were fitted in later models, and also which parts are needed to make it all work. With a change of engine there will probably be a change in weight so factor in new springs to suit.

Older Defenders with NA or TD

Mr Buxton admires his supercharged Jaguar V8; not content with standard engines, he went for something completely different.

diesels can be converted to receive the 200Tdi engine, improving performance, reliability, and economy in one go. A few bolt holes aren't present in the 200Tdi flywheel housing and these can either be drilled or replaced with the old NA/TD housing. There are adaptor pipes available to mate the Tdi exhaust down pipe to the older Defender exhaust system, and pipes will need to be made up to run to the intercooler. If using a Discovery radiator and intercooler pack, the old Defender radiator mounts need to be dropped down to make it fit. The Tdi visco fan hits the steering box so most people remove it and fit an electric fan. The 300Tdi is a similar swap, although the engine mounts are substantially different so most conversions use Discovery mounts welded onto the chassis. Converting a Range Rover to either of these engines is fairly similar, too, except that the bulkhead overhangs the rocker cover; which means that the bulkhead must be modified to be able to remove the rocker cover. In addition, the steering box on some models can foul the engine and needs to be swapped for a later design.

In South America a variant of the 300Tdi is made under licence by International Engines. Designated HS 2.8l TGV, this redesigned unit has been taken out to 2.8-litres and produces an easy 135bhp and 375Nm. To make it fit in a Land Rover there are a few modifications needed: some of the un-drilled bolt holes must be

drilled and tapped; the oil filter has to be moved; it needs an adaptor for the crank to flywheel due to the different crank design; the dipstick tube has to be relocated to avoid hitting the front prop; and, finally, the turbo and exhaust pipes are all in the wrong place so need modified parts. The high torque is too much for the standard 242mm clutch, so either a heavy-duty cover plate or a larger clutch is required. Other than that, it's a bolt-in swap!

Even more diesel power can be had by fitting a TD5, but this is a much bigger job. As well as needing engine mounts welding on the chassis, it requires: an in-tank fuel pump; the full engine wiring loom and ECU; the intake system with the air flow meter; clutch position switch; electronic accelerator pedal assembly; fuel cut-off-switch; and transfer box selector sensors. Most conversions use the whole TD5 engine and transmission assembly with the Defender TD5 gearbox mount. Early Range Rovers will need the transmission tunnel modifying to the later size. The ECU has a built-in immobiliser function that normally talks to the body control module (BCM). Fitting a BCM is a huge job but it can be replaced by an aftermarket communications box, such as the Rovacom or Nanocom, making it a whole lot easier. It's a fair old job but with massive tuning potential it can be worth it.

The BMW diesel, as fitted in the P38a Range Rover, is another option, using the P38a gearbox mated to the Classic transfer box. Again, it needs all the electrical systems bringing over from the donor car in a similar way to the TD5, but where the Range Rover used the 2.5-litre engine, BMW had variations up to 3-litre which can be tuned up to well over 200bhp. To use the BMW 3-litre engine from a 530d or similar car the sump and ancillaries from the

To mate the Jaguar V8 to the Range Rover gearbox a thick alloy adaptor plate is used.

Cars with air-con already have an electric fan.

Oil cooler kits can help if the car is worked very hard.

Range Rover version must be fitted. So, although complex, this conversion does open up quite a few possibilities.

Fitting an engine from another manufacturer is a much bigger job. If the original gearbox is to be used an adaptor plate has to be made to join the engine block to the bell housing, then the flywheel is adapted to take the new clutch or torque converter. After that, the engine mounts must be fabricated, exhaust adapted, intake system built, and electrics redesigned. The bulkhead often has to be remodelled to allow for the starter or exhaust, and the oil filter mountings and sump have to be modified to avoid the front axle at full articulation.

For many, these challenges are part of the fun, and a number of alternative engines have found their way into these magnificent cars:

The Jaguar/Land Rover V8 is an interesting option. The engine first appeared in 1996 in 4.0-litre form and has since been produced in 3.2-, 3.5-, 4.2- and 4.4-litre capacities. There were a number of detail changes brought in when the 4.2- and 4.4-litre came out, improving reliability and performance. The 4.0 and 4.2 are also available in supercharged form, the 4.2-litre producing 420bhp as standard. These are relatively lightweight (205-225kg) and reasonably compact engines. A Discovery 3 sump will be needed with a modification to clear the Classic front differential at full bump. For more on this conversion see the example in chapter 10.

For real power at a very reasonable price, a good modern V8 is the Corvette LS3, with over 500bhp possible and a wealth of tuning parts from the USA race scene. The iron block adds about 100kg but the all alloy version is only 20kg heavier than the Rover unit.

ENGINE COOLING

Standard radiators work well as long as enough air flows through them. Mud plastered over the matrix drastically reduces cooling ability so some people fit splash guards when mud plugging to direct some of it away from the radiator. In Comp Safari races it's commonplace to put the radiator behind the cab and duct air down to it from the roof top.

Where cars are expected to spend a lot of time at very low speeds, electric fans can provide maximum airflow at any engine speed. They can also be fitted with an override switch to either permanently engage them to reduce under bonnet temperature or to disengage them when wading. One of the problems with an engine driven fan is evident when driving through deep water. The fan blades can be damaged as they strike the water surface and cause the belt to fail under the very high load.

Cars fitted with air-conditioning already have electric fans that can be wired up to an additional temperature switch to replace the mechanical fan in all but the hottest climates.

Interestingly, some cars only ever used at low speeds have been converted to have the fan blowing forwards – blowing any potential blockage away from the radiator – although it's uncertain how effective this was.

EXHAUST

Apart from performance tuning, the main reason for modifying the exhaust is to avoid it being damaged in heavy off-road situations. The main problem on all models is that the tail pipe can be crushed when the back of the car drops into a gully. A solution is to make the exhaust

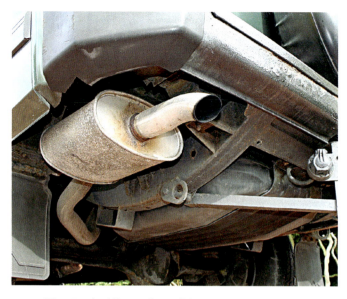

The standard Range Rover/Discovery-style exhaust.

This D44 pipe removes the rear box on Defender 90s and bobtails.

A side exit exhaust is less vulnerable than the standard one.

exit through the side panel, just behind the rear wheel: a large diameter hole is cut in the side panel to allow for exhaust movement.

The standard exhaust does a fine job of keeping the car quiet, but if you fancy a more fruity note there are plenty of options. The middle silencer is a labyrinth type designed to remove the low frequency basey sounds – the sort of sounds that many enthusiasts quite like! So replacing this with a section of tube can bring out that V8 burble or diesel rumble without being excessively loud. The rear silencer is a straight through absorption type unit and its job

is to take out the higher frequency sounds and stop resonances building up that make the cabin vibrate and boom. Removing it brings more sound out in a generally pleasant way but there may be some speeds where it resonates and gets a bit annoying.

Using a Land Rover off-road means the exhaust gets a hard time. The standard mild steel system can corrode, usually along the tube seam and round all the welds. A stainless system will be a lot more resilient, but look out for cheap ones welded with ordinary steel MIG wire so the joins still rust out. In addition, there are many grades of stainless and cheaper varieties corrode almost as fast as a mild steel system. The final point regarding stainless systems is that the metal is harder than mild steel and, where a mild steel tube makes a fairly dull thud, a stainless one will ring when struck, so the overall sound can be a little more 'tinny,' although it's not hugely noticeable.

ENGINE MOUNTS

In extreme off-road situations the weight of the engine and gearbox bouncing about can cause the mounts to be ripped apart. Competition cars often use the 'cotton reel' type captive mounts, which, as well as being much firmer, prevent the mount separating in the event of the rubber failing. They work much like two links in a chain; one part

Competition 'cotton reel' engine mounts are very strong but transmit lots of noise into the cab.

feeding through the other with rubber filling the joint.

TRANSMISSION AND PROPS

The Range Rover was originally fitted with a quaint LT95 combined four-speed gearbox and transfer box – simple, solid, and reliable. In about 1984, it switched to a separate transfer box with a Rover LT77 five-speed gearbox, as used on the Rover SD1 range. Initially, the suffix D gearboxes tended to wear out, and a series of revisions ensued: suffix F had a larger layshaft; the G model had stronger gear teeth and a bigger oil pump to cope with the oil cooled versions, such as the North American Spec D90; then there was the suffix H, also known as the LT77S, which had a revised 'double synchro' system, that in reality made little difference. The LT77 gearbox was redesigned heavily for greater strength and better gear changes to become the R380. Its 5th gear housing at the back of the box is 30mm longer than an LT77 so it's not a direct replacement. However, as Land Rover wanted to use the R380 for service replacement on older LT77 cars it developed a special short bell housing

version, which is worth knowing if you are considering an upgrade or making a very short special – the bell housing and input shaft can be retrofitted to existing R380 'boxes, too. The R380 can also be found in some TVRs and LDV vans so there are plenty secondhand units about, although bell housings and input shafts are designed specially for the application and won't directly fit a Land Rover. Despite the stronger input bearing, the R380 tends to lose synchro on 2nd and baulk when changing into 4th. Both issues require a rebuild, but can be lived with temporarily. Both gearboxes went through a number of detail revisions; the serial number on the side of the box will indicate which version it is.

Suffix L R380s are the best, and the R380 also has the provision for an oil cooler which can improve reliability for heavy competition use. Either 'box, if in good condition, should cope with about 300bhp.

Early Defender V8 cars had the Santana L185 'box, distinguished by its ally casing – which is stronger still, but getting quite rare.

That last gearbox to be used came in 2007 when the Defender received the Ford Transit engine and the Getrag Ford Transmissions (GFT) MT82 six-speed, still driving the trusty LT230 transfer box via a fairly long adaptor housing. This gearbox doesn't fit the older Land Rover engines but does open up the possibility of using other Ford engines.

Auto 'boxes have always been reliable, and can be used as clutchless manuals for competition use as long as the oil is cool and in good condition.

The original LT95 four-speed manual with integral transfer box, which also incorporates the handbrake lever.

An R380 with an almost identical main cast casing to the LT77, but with a longer ally fifth gear housing.

The ZF auto is favoured in high speed competition; seen here with the LT230 transfer box. (Courtesy Devon 4x4)

the medium converter fits in a TD5 bell housing but the 300Tdi needs to use a modified V8 unit.

The ZF4HP24EH and 22EH 'box fitted to the Discovery 2 was electronically controlled, which brings up a few possibilities. When combined with a programmable ECU, such as Compushift, you can not only have very smooth auto shifts just where you want them, but you can also make a paddle shift manual mode and lock-up the converter clutch to get better low speed control off-road. It really is the best of both worlds.

Additionally, the stronger parts from the middle of the later 4HP24 can be retrofitted to the Range Rover's standard 4HP22 to strengthen it.

For higher power engines with more than about 400bhp, it may be more cost effective to swap to a big American auto, such as the GM TH400, which are cheap secondhand and can be fitted with proper race internals.

On high power manual cars there are a few popular conversions including: the Toyota; Borg Warner T5 or six-speed T6; and the Tremek TKO600, which is pricey but couples nicely to a Corvette 600bhp motor should you so wish.

TRANSFER BOX

The standard transfer box is either the LT230 (Leyland Transmissions, 230mm between shafts) with a lockable centre diff or the Borg-Warner unit with a visco centre. The LT230 is better in serious off-road applications and racing, where the visco unit can boil up and explode. For road use, the Borg-Warner unit reduces wheel spin when you pull out of a T-junction at full tilt. It's quite straightforward to swap between the two types of transfer box to suit your project.

The LT230 came in a range of high ratio gears, with the tallest gearing found

Early models had a Chrysler three-speed unit, which is solid but harsh. The ZF 4HP22 four-speed was introduced in 1985, which is very smooth and has been used for up to 300bhp.

The ZF had three possible torque converters with different lock-up speeds that can be interchanged to get the right response for your project.

The small one is used on the standard 300Tdi, P38a diesel, and TD5 auto and helps improve fuel economy, but by only a small amount. Unfortunately, the small diameter means

that the lock-up clutch struggles to cope with even mildly tuned engines. But the main problem is the relatively high stall speed which unfortunately means that all that low down torque cannot be used – it's quite annoying to drive.

Far better is the medium-sized torque converter, as fitted to most of the V8s, except the early 4.6-litre P38a. This allows the diesels to lug from lower speeds and gives better off-road control, as well as being stronger.

Obviously, fitting a bigger torque converter needs a bigger bell housing:

The LT230 transfer box incorporates a diff lock and two gears for high and low range.

This output shaft on an R380 gearbox shows the spline wear common on early diesels. The transfer box splines were similarly worn.

in the V8 Range Rover. Standard ratios are approximately 1.0:1, 1.2:1, 1.4:1, and 1.6:1, although there were four variations on the 1.2 gear set from 1.192 up to 1.222, but this is a very slight change.

To work out which is best for your project you can calculate the engine speed relative to the road speed using the following formula:

mph per 1000rpm = (2.976xD) / (GxTxR)

Where:

D = Tyre diameter in inches, calculated from 2 x rolling radius.

G = Gear ratio, such as 4th 1.00 or 5th 0.77.

T = Transfer box ratio.

R = Differential Ratio, usually 3.54.

Changing the diff can make it a more capable unit. ARB make an air locking unit which does pretty much the same thing as the manual diff lock; Quaife make an Automatic Torque Biasing diff which runs the most power to the axle with the most grip. Some racers use Kam diffs, or a fully-locked

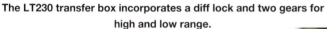

diff and a variety of gears. For specials, shorter output housings from Rakeway Ltd reduce length by 70mm.

For purpose-built off-road racers the transfer box can be replaced completely by a custom-made race box. These usually have just one gear set in, but boxes such as the Milner 'Quick Change' allow the gear sets to be changed relatively easily to suit the intended purpose of the car.

Many racers put the engine in the back for best weight distribution,

The central link – the hidden secret in a double Cardon prop joint – keeps both UJs under control and at the same angle.

which means the direction of the propshaft rotation has to be reversed, or the diffs inverted in the axles.

Companies such as Milner and Rakeway offer reverse rotation transfer boxes which do not have an intermediate gear, thus making them smaller, lighter, and stronger but the straight cut gears are quite noisy.

On diesels, the shaft between the R380 gearbox and the transfer box can wear, leading to rattling and eventually complete failure due to oil starvation. However, this was redesigned and the revised part can be retrofitted.

If you have the old four-speed L95

gearbox you can change to a later five-speed one as long as you take it from the same type of vehicle because the Defender and Range Rover units have different selector mechanisms. You will need to take it complete with the LT230 transfer box and gearbox mountings.

PROPSHAFTS

An uprated vehicle puts greater strain on the propshafts, and lifted cars can push the joints through much greater angles than the standard shafts were ever designed for. Wider yokes at the UJ allow for a greater angle and larger bearings to be used, but any Hookes type joint will vibrate at speed when running at high angles. The solution is to use a double Hooke (double Cardon) joint, which has two UJs back-to-back with a spherical link joining the two to stop the whole joint flopping to one side. Another solution is to use a wide angle CV joint, such as the Lobro favoured in rallying circles.

AXLES

The standard axle does a fine job, but in extreme conditions with heavy loading it can deform. A common strengthening method is to run tie straps of thick steel

A strengthened D44 axle with a tough alloy pan. (Courtesy Devon 4x4)

from the hub end of the axle casing down to the bottom of the diff pan, triangulating the assembly but reducing ground clearance very slightly. On the front axle the casing slims down just inboard of the swivel housing and can be a weak point. Strengthened casings are available to solve this issue and can be combined with stronger diff protection in re-engineered axles such as those from Devon 4x4.

To some extent, most axles are interchangeable with those from other models. The exceptions are: the Defender rear axle with Salisbury diff or drum brakes; and the early two-door Range Rover rear axle with the damper mounted behind the axle on one side, and ahead of the axle on the other (also, this Range Rover's front axle had narrower radius arms). As already mentioned, there was also a small change to wheel centres on the hub when alloy wheels came in.

Cars with anti-roll bars had brackets welded onto the axle casings – these can be fabricated for older axles and welded-on if needed.

DIFFS

The same basic unit has been in service with Land Rover since the Series days. Whilst it's a good standard unit, its limitations soon become apparent. The main issue is the differential internals: there are usually only two drive pinion gears and their

The air locking diff can be seen in this D44 axle. Note the copper-coloured air tube. (Courtesy Devon 4x4)

This diff has suffered from input shaft bearing wear. The pinion has been eaten away, until eventually drive was lost. Uprated items remedy this.

mounting shafts are relatively small. Some later Defender 110s had four pinion differentials, which, obviously, have double the strength. Ashcroft transmissions offer a further upgrade based on this four pin diff, but with bigger cross pin and a very strong housing.

Another issue is that the gear teeth on the crown wheel are ground at an angle that makes them stronger when driven in one direction, so the rear diff lasts longer than the front diff, but this does mean that a common diff can be used in both axles.

Quaife Automatic Torque Biasing differentials channel more torque to the wheel with the most traction. In very slippery conditions there may not be enough grip for the unit to work effectively, but for most mud, rock, and gravel terrain they work exceptionally well. The Detroit Trutrack is a relatively cheap alternative popular in Comp Safari racing.

All models use the same diff ratio of 3.54:1, but some older series Land Rovers used 4.70, which is a little better for low speed work like rock crawling. Companies such as Ashcroft Transmissions offer a range of ratios to suit different applications.

HALF SHAFTS

For most of the vehicles' existence the half shafts have had a relatively course spline into the diff, which under extreme loading can break and leave a stub of shaft stuck in the diff. Later shafts had a finer spline and are less prone to snapping. These came in around 1994, and can be retrofitted to earlier axles by transferring over the diff and hub drive plate, although it's usually easier to just swap a whole axle.

The fine spline shafts are not indestructible and custom-made thicker shafts may be needed for heavy competition use. One thing to consider, though, is that if the drive train is overloaded for some reason, a broken half shaft is a lot easier to repair than a broken diff or gearbox. Some racers consider it to be like a mechanical equivalent of a fuse protecting the more expensive parts of the transmission.

6x6

Over the years there have been a number of six-wheel variants; Land Rover's own version starts out as a Defender 130 and has an extra rear portion of chassis welded-in. Not all six-wheelers are six-wheel drive. Many, such as the Carmichael airport fire tenders, use the third axle just for carrying extra weight and it's not driven, making it a 6x4.

Most conversions that are 6x6 drive the extra rear axle by taking drive through the middle axle: either by having a second shaft chain or gear driven off the input shaft; or by using another diff nose attached to the rear of the axle driven off the crown wheel. The former allows for a longer drive shaft to the rear axle and doesn't limit articulation as much as the latter solution.

The factory 6x6 option used a through drive unit on the middle axle and a short prop to the rear axle.

PORTAL AXLES

These axles have the wheel hub centre a few inches below the axle centre and a gear set in the hub to take the drive from the half shaft down to the wheel hub. This means that the axle and differential are higher up, improving ground clearance.

The portal axle from a Volvo C303 uses Land Rover propshaft flanges, but everything else will have to be modified.

Portal axles were fitted to a number of other vehicles, such as the Unimog, but those from the Volvo C303 range of military vehicles have the advantage that the diff is on the right-hand side (Unimogs are on the left), and the diff drive flange is the same as the Land Rover item, so Land Rover propshafts bolt on without modification. The Volvo axle was designed for leaf springs so brackets for the Land Rover suspension must be welded-on. The other issue is that these axles have large drum brakes and, whilst if in good order they're reasonably good at stopping a car (the C303 was half a ton heavier than a Discovery with a high load rating), many owners prefer disc brakes, especially if they wish to retain ABS. Fitting Land Rover disc brakes to the Volvo axle is possible with various adaptors, although portal axle cars usually run very large diameter tyres so that brake force will be reduced considerably, unless proportionally larger discs are used, too.

The wheel hubs take 8-stud 20in wheels, so there's more expense to be considered in the tyre department.

WADING

Splashing through lots of water is fun – it may be seen as childish by some but they're probably just jealous because they can't do it! Land Rovers were designed to cope with fording up to 0.5m as standard, but can be modified to run when almost completely submerged. Some of the river crossings in the Camel Trophy were driven with water up to the roof, driver sitting on the window sill so that his head was above the waterline.

There are a number of things to consider when wading. The engine must be kept running by feeding it air from a roof-mounted snorkel, and sealing any possible leakage points. Then it's a matter of stopping water getting into the oily bits, including the engine, gearbox, axles, hubs, and transfer box. Finally, all the electrics have to be protected from moisture getting into connectors and control boxes. After wading, the car needs to be thoroughly dried out, usually with a long drive – parking up a wet car results in all sorts of things seizing up and corroding.

Snorkels

The basic idea is that the inlet pipe for the air filter is extended by a snorkel tube to the top of the roof. The end of the tube needs a guard to stop debris and rain being drawn into it and blocking the filter. Most kits have an inlet that can be fitted facing either forwards, which rams air in at speed and may give a small enhancement to performance, or backwards to protect it from overhanging foliage or flying dirt. The tube goes through the wing on its way to the air filter: most systems use two parts which are bonded onto each side of the wing panel after a suitable hole has been cut. Most standard air filters have a small rubber valve underneath to allow moisture to escape, and the filter housings usually have a fairly light seal. Obviously, when submerged, these would leak water into the filter, so a watertight filter

Preparing the car for wading requires breathers on axles, a plug in the bell housing, and many other modifications.

A typical snorkel with a movable intake at the top; aimed forward for a small ram air effect on the motorway and turned backwards to prevent water ingress.

This is taking wading to extremes; note the bubbles coming from this Camel Trophy Discovery as it drives on the river bed. (Courtesy Land Rover)

housing is needed. Another option is to fit the filter on the top of the snorkel tube on the roof, doing away with the engine bay filter completely, but this will leave the filter vulnerable to damage.

To make the Rover V8 and older petrol engines resistant to ignition failure in water, you first need to decide just how waterproof your engine has to be. It's vital that the basic parts of the system are in good order. Good quality

The V8 distributor has two breather holes in the base that cause the engine to stall in water, so fitting tubes to them is a top wading modification.

8mm silicone leads should be fine (even 30000-volt systems won't arc through that much silicone). Make sure the boots at each end are very tightly fitting. With new sparkplugs, the new leads should fit with a water tight seal; old leads go hard and will leak here. The same goes for the distributor cap, which should also be a good quality standard item – check it fits the casing well, and put some silicone grease round the base of it to help the seal. Spray all the low tension connectors with contact grease to prevent corrosion.

The distributor has two breather holes in the casing just below the advance weights. These holes are very important as they prevent a build of crank case gasses (which leak up the distributor shaft) that could otherwise blow the distributor apart.

If, when Green Laning, you have problems with the engine spluttering every time you go fording, chances are a small amount of moisture is getting through the breather holes, possibly thrown up by the crank pulley, and causing a bit of arcing in the distributor cap. In most cases, a simple splash

guard will direct the water away from this area.

When driving through water quickly (such as in a Comp Safari race) it gets everywhere in the engine bay, so the breathers need to be extended. The holes may be fitted with 2BA breather nipples that have the threads cut down to about 1.6mm to avoid fouling the advance weights – always check on your distributor how much clearance you have. Because the metal is so thin, the nipples need to be bonded in. The breathers are then connected via small bore tubing to tappings; one just down stream of the throttle to draw gas out of the distributor, and one between the throttle and air filter to let clean air in. With it all assembled and sealed you should, apparently, be able to throw a bucket of water at the engine without it missing a beat.

If the water line will be above the top of the engine you have the additional problem of condensation and water seeping under pressure through every joint in the system. This means there's also a need to bond in and seal the electrical connection on the distributor, as well as the joint between the vacuum advance unit and the distributor body. Some vacuum advance units have a breather hole which will have to be connected to fresh air via a pipe.

If you are doing this sort of work you will, by now, have many breather pipes (rocker covers, axle etc) but don't be tempted to join them together as a small pressure change will effect timing. The Silicone sealant around the distributor cap bonding it to the base will need replacing each time you take the cap off.

Water can also enter the engine through all the leaking gaskets, so a complete strip down and carefully fitted and sealed new gaskets is absolutely

necessary for this kind of use. The same applies to the diesel engines, and the gearbox, too.

Early cars had simple button-type axle breathers that, unfortunately, let water in. Later cars had breather tubes on both axles, and on the transfer box, which go up just above the chassis line. These can be extended for serious wading and joined into the snorkel. If water is going to be above the bonnet line the engine breathers and both the engine and gearbox dip stick tubes must be extended, too.

BODY AND INTERIOR
The Land Rover body is separate from the chassis and this opens up all sorts of possibilities. For example, one way of getting more clearance for the wheels in the arches and raising bodywork out of the way of obstacles is with a body lift, which involves fitting raised blocks in the mounts between the body and chassis. Although ramp over angles and ground clearance are not improved, it does allow more space for increased

White plastic blocks raise this Discovery body a few inches to give better clearance to the big tyres.

axle articulation. Body lifts are usually only one or two inches in height.

The Discovery and Range Rover bodies have many similarities so a number of parts, such as doors, are interchangeable. In fact, some people have put complete Range Rover front ends on Discoveries just to make something different. The bulkhead and floorpan of the Discovery is very similar to that of a four-door Range Rover and they share the same windscreen, the main difference being the scuttle at the base of the screen. So many parts of the interior are also interchangeable. The last Range Rovers had a 'soft dash' based on the Discovery 300 unit which offers dual-zone heating and a more ergonomic layout. Fitting a 300 dash and heater into an early Range rover is a big job as there a number of brackets and fixings that need to be adapted or created, but it can be done.

Defender bodies, by contrast, have no shared parts with the other two coil-sprung cars. Instead, it's based on the old Series Land Rover, and some people have used older parts to make a more traditional-looking Land Rover but with the advantages of the coil-sprung chassis.

Early Discovery seats may not be the most comfortable to many, but Range Rover seats can be fitted to the 200-style models as a straight swap. 300 models need an adaptor plate due to the different runner spacing.

The Defender has very rudimentary seats and upgrading them is very tempting. There are a range of bolt-on upgrades available from companies such as Exmoor Trim.

Seats form part of the safety equipment in a car and need to be secure enough to stay intact and not break free in an accident. The mountings of a seat take a huge force in a front or rear end crash: as the body

This Discovery 300 has comfy Range Rover seats, which required a substantial adaptor plate to match the different bolt patterns.

Four-point competition harnesses use a central seatbelt-type buckle, making getting in and out relatively easy ... (Courtesy Devon 4x4)

moves forward there is no extra force on the seat mounts, but as the body rebounds backwards the back of the seat is put under great force, which tends to make the seat pivot over its rear mounting points and pull the front mounts upwards out of their bases – that's why seats and mounts have to be very sturdy.

Because of the simple layout of the

seat mounting it's possible to fabricate a mounting system for pretty much any seat, but whatever system is employed it must strong and durable. It's not reasonable to simply bolt a flat piece of ally sheet down as an adaptor to other seat bases because it will simply rip apart in an accident and leave the occupant bouncing round the interior.

If the car is going to do serious

off-road work it may be worth fitting 'bucket'-style competition seats. These are a single piece so there's no back adjustment, but it does mean they're much stronger and lighter than standard seats. They provide excellent side support and keep the driver steady, even on very uneven ground. Because they're bucket-like, the base tends to fill up with any dirt or mud that the occupant had on their cloths – removable seat cushions and removable seat covers make cleaning easier. Because the occupant tends to slide into the seat, the side bar nearest the door gets a lot of wear. Seats are available with a durable covering on the high wear areas and vinyl coverings are also available, making the whole seat more tolerant to mud – these can be very hot and sweaty on long drives or in hot weather.

Fitting race-type harnesses is a popular modification that can add significant safety if done correctly, but there are some very important factors that must be understood in order to prevent them being less safe than standard seatbelts.

Simply brilliant pieces of

... compared to this Tomcat with six-point harnesses that require each strap to be separately clipped into the quick-release buckle – this can be a bit fiddly.

Finding somewhere secure enough to attach the shoulder straps can be a problem. This neat device bolts solidly to the roll cage and then ...

engineering, in a crash, seatbelts restrain the occupant to ensure they decelerate with the car, rather than continuing and stopping much more abruptly against the dash or screen. In order for this to work the belt must be tight against the body, otherwise the body will continue forwards until it hits the belt, resulting in higher peak forces.

The mounting points must be able to take the huge forces of an accident, which can easily exceed several tons. The exact method depends on the belt design, so look at the manufacturers recommendations.

The other thing that needs to be dealt with is the angle that the shoulder straps make. If they slope downwards, such that the mounts are below shoulder level, then in a crash they will pull down on your shoulders, and could crush your

spine – so you'll want to avoid that one! Most manufacturers recommend an angle of less than 45 degrees, but the seat should also provide sturdy harness guides that protect the spine.

The lap belt must be mounted so that it goes across the pelvis: if it can ride up then all the stopping force gets applied to your soft organs, which is dangerous. That's why race harnesses have a crotch strap to pull the lap belt down.

... bolts through the rear bulkhead to the shoulder strap fitting.

Race harnesses have to be adjusted to fit tightly every time you put them on. There's a temptation to leave them loose for ease of use but this ruins their effectiveness. You can now get inertia reel harnesses which are a bit more costly but a lot easier to use everyday.

For real competition vehicles you have to use approved harnesses that have a manufacturing date sewn in – they're only allowed to be used for a few years to ensure they're in peak condition. If you are building a competition car, consult your regulations carefully for details.

When competition harnesses go out of date they're often sold on for non-competition use. Although they can seem like a bargain, if they have been used in competition they will have been constantly pulled about and will be weaker, and if they have been in a crash then they may be even weaker than a standard seatbelt.

With off-road use mud gets into the webbing of the harness and the microscopic grit particles cut into its fibres. It's very difficult to see this because it's happening inside the fabric. So if you get the harness muddy it has to be removed and cleaned as soon as possible.

For these reasons, and as they're not very expensive new, avoid buying secondhand harnesses.

It's very unusual for a car to catch fire, but as it's always a possibility it's worth carrying a fire extinguisher. As with any heavy items it needs to be secured so that it can't whack you on the head in an accident.

If you are going to play on rough tracks in the middle of nowhere, it's a good idea to fit a quality first aid kit somewhere easy to reach in an emergency.

Visibility off-road is crucial, but, as mentioned, it's not a good idea to use windscreen wipers to remove mud because the grit in it scratches the screen. Over time this can ruin the surface finish and make night driving difficult.

The trick is to use water jets to rinse most of the mud off, and the wipers only when the muddy terrain has been safely passed. One way of doing this is to use the power jets normally fitted in the bumper to wash the headlights, complete with its larger pump and tank, and have both jets pointing in front of the driver to clear a spot big enough to see out, operated on a separate switch so it can be used independently of the wipers. Another neat trick is to plumb the normal washer jets on to the wiper arms, so that it squirts water directly in front of the wiper blade, this way the blade is never pushing dry grit across the screen.

However, even with these precautions, a well used off-roader will get scratches on the screen. Luckily, there's a simple solution as the scratches are usually very small. A good glass polish and a lot of hard work will bring it back to good condition.

Heated mirrors can be a real help on cold mornings and are relatively simple to fit. The heated mirror glass can be bonded straight over the existing mirror glass or the old glass can be removed. The wiring uses a relay with a fused supply from the battery and is triggered by taking a splice off the heated rear window switch.

The Defender interior heater is a little weak as standard and doesn't demist the side windows effectively. There are a number of aftermarket replacements available and the simplest solution is to fit revised ducting and nozzles. Removing the dashboard trim allows access to the existing screen vents. These can be replaced with larger items and extra ducting fitted that runs along the bulkhead to the side panels, which need holes cut in to allow the fitting of nozzles for side window demisting.

This still relies on the standard

Getting modern air-con climate control into a Defender is tricky. However, now that Land Rover has put it in production, retrofitting is an option. (Courtesy Land Rover)

blower and heater, which in many cases will still do the job. More powerful units are available, providing better heating in extreme weather and higher air flow rate for improved demisting.

Air-conditioning is an option for the Defender, either by fitting an aftermarket system or by retrofitting the system from a late model car. It's a big job but, as well as keeping things cool on a hot day, it drastically improves demisting, particularly useful after wading or when everyone has just got back in the car with damp coats on a rainy day.

The door window glass is quite tall on all models, and when the runners have worn slightly there's more play. When winding the window up the glass can be pulled outward by air pressure when travelling at speed, making it difficult to close. Most models have a small plastic wedge in the outer part of the frame to guide the glass back into the channel seal, which can be retrofitted to older models as long as the glass channel seal is in good order. An alternative is to fit a suction cup to the top of the glass, allowing it to be pulled manually inward.

Secure stowage for things like maps, torches, tools, etc is usually very handy. The standard stowage on most models is fairly poor, though, with open bins that lose their contents in rough terrain. Interior stowage was probably most thought about in the Discovery, which had roof-mounted map nets and door bins, but even this has limitations when compared to most saloon cars. The good news is that several companies produce storage solutions, and the bins and nets from other models can be added to augment an

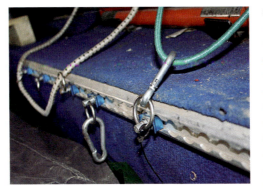

These handy strips allow loads to be secured easily with simple clip-in retaining points.

Discovery rear seatbelt bolts have been replaced with FIA-approved race harness eye bolts, making securing loads easy. The Discovery also has two extra bolt points at the rear load bed for this purpose.

existing system. One popular modification is adding a central cubby box, particularly useful on Defenders where it replaces the uncomfortable centre seat.

ROOF RACK, ROOF TENT

Expedition vehicles can generate a significant increase in load space by fitting a roof rack, but there are some problems. The body structure at roof level was never very

strong on Range Rover and Defender models, and, although the Discovery had substantial strengthening in the C- and D-pillars and a steel roof, which is significantly stronger, if heavy loads are to be taken on the roof all require the mounting points to spread the load evenly through the roof rails, usually by having multiple mounting points. The manufacturer's roof loading maximum figure should not be exceeded, and this limit must include the weight of the roof rack. If the roof rack mounts onto an external roll cage the forces are transmitted directly into the chassis and

This Defender has exhaust U-clamps bolted through the gutters to secure light roof loads.

A substantial roof rack with five sturdy mounting points on each side to spread the load.

heavier loads may be taken. Although in all cases, putting heavy loads on the roof de-stabilises the car and makes it significantly more likely to roll. Lifting heavy loads off the roof also presents a risk of falling or being crushed. In summary, don't put heavy things on the roof.

A roof rack also increases drag and fuel consumption at speed, so if it's not needed take it off.

Having said all that, a roof rack on an expedition or camping trip is an ideal place to store bulky yet lightweight items such as tents, bicycles, and canoes.

Rear ladders are very handy for getting loads onto a roof rack. On a Discovery they simply bolt onto the rear door, and on Defenders they bolt to rear panel next to the door. Range Rovers present a problem, due to the way the tailgate opens, so either a foldaway ladder is needed or simply a two-step attached to the lower tailgate only, after all the roof isn't that high on a Range Rover.

There are some other simpler modifications, such as fitting mud flap ties. When reversing on rough terrain the mud flap can get caught between the tyre and an obstacle, which rips it off. If the flap is tied up when driving off-road then it's saved. This requires a reliable fitting to be installed into the flap as just cutting into it will lead to it ripping in use. The mounting hole should have a smooth rim and the fitting must spread the loading evenly. Then a suitable hooking point just needs to be installed onto the body.

LIGHTS

Good lights are essential. The standard lights can be very good if well-maintained but there comes a point in off-road situations when you need a bit more.

Roof lights complement the high power, uprated 7in classic headlights to improve off-road night visibility.

Kits are available to improve the performance of 7in headlights. These were once a standard fitment on a huge range of cars around the world.

Most models are fitted with the old industry standard 7in round units. As ever, there are cheap replacements and there are good replacements, but no good cheap ones. The reflector and lens quality is vital, and the variation between budget brands and quality brands is huge. So, if your standard units seem inadequate under normal driving situations, the first step is to fit decent replacements. Unfortunately, the Discovery doesn't have these standard lamps so it's a bit more complicated. The 200-style light was taken from the Sherpa van, which was adequate at best, while the 300-style had properly-designed unique lamps that can offer a small upgrade in lighting performance on a 200 car. Again, if the standard lamps are not performing under normal road conditions then the chances are they need replacing with quality new units.

In both cases, the second upgrade is to fit modern high-performance bulbs. There have been a number of technical advances in the last ten years which make modern standard replacement bulbs

Upgrading a Discovery 200 with 300-style lights also requires the matching indicators and trim,

Modern bulbs are hugely more efficient than the original units – the cheapest lighting upgrade.

Auxiliary lights can be designed for different purposes, such as long-range or wide-angle; positioning is crucial for getting the best use from them.

switches on with main beam. Fitting them on the roof provides extra height and range, casting slightly less shadow close up, although they will illuminate the bonnet which can ruin your night vision.

Often in off-road situations you need a good view of the road to the side, where a tight turn is to be negotiated or obstacles need to be avoided. A lamp with a wider beam is needed to illuminate these areas, either a driving light or a fog light angled to the side. Mounting a set of lights on the edge of the roof can be an advantage here, as it illuminates the terrain directly to the side of the car, too. You can even get door mirror mounted lights that illuminate the side, but don't put glaring light on the bonnet.

In the UK, it's illegal to use a light that can be moved by hand from inside the car, but such a light can be very useful on roads outside of the UK to investigate specific areas ahead.

When off-road you sometimes have to reverse out of a sticky situation, so fitting a higher power reversing light triggered by the standard reverse lamp via a relay can be beneficial. It's best mounted high up to get a good view of the road behind.

Lights on the roof are vulnerable to being struck by overhanging branches. They should be mounted to allow them to fold back rather than break off, and preferably have some form of protection bar.

For cars used mainly on-road, roof-mounted lights increase drag significantly and adversely effect fuel consumption.

Auxiliary lights should be wired in using their own fused supply from the

Rear lights on specials often use trailer spares, but these custom D44 units set off this tray-back superbly.

battery via relays linked to the auxiliary or ignition feed from the key switch. One way of doing this is to have the relay coil connected to power via the key switch and earth via the lamp switch. Spot and driving lights should be linked to the main beam signal via relay so that on dipped beam they're off.

RECOVERY
Winches and bumpers

Fitting a winch is relatively easy if using a professionally made winch bumper but there are some disadvantages. The extra weight, particularly if using steel cable, adversely affects handling, load capacity, braking distance, and fuel consumption. Most winch bumpers will stick out a bit further and reduce approach or departure angle. There's also a safety issue – it's a big hard lump of metal sticking out the front of the car. If your main use for the car is the school run then consider other options.

One option is to keep the original bumper and swap over to the winch bumper before an off-road trip. In addition to the normal winch parts, you would need a high current electrical connector to allow the winch motor to be disconnected easily.

When selecting a winch consider

up to 90 per cent brighter than original items.

No matter how good the standard lights are, there are some situations off-road where they don't point in the direction you need. Sometimes, on a dark night in the middle of now where, where the terrain doesn't reflect anything, it's almost like the light is being sucked out of the standard beams and the amount of road illuminated seems tiny. Long-range high power spot lamps can help, mounted on the front bumper and connected with a relay that

Sometimes the only way to get out is with a winch! Essential equipment on this Camel Trophy Defender 110. (Courtesy Land Rover)

be used for extended periods the heat issue goes away, too. As ever, it's a matter of choosing the right tool for the job.

A small lightweight winch doesn't necessarily mean less pulling power. By using pulley blocks you can double up the pulling power, in fact, with a pulley block on the front bumper and two attached to your anchor point, you can get four times the pull force. It will only travel a quarter of the distance, but

The winch here is mounted behind the bumper, which reduces front protrusion, but means the grille must be modified to fit it.

This rear winch has a solid fairlead, synthetic rope, and substantial recovery eyes securely welded-on – ideal for doubling up the rope via a pulley.

There are many types of rope, and the right choice depends on the application. This synthetic rope is very strong and light.

that's usually enough to get you out of a hole.

There are three main types of winch, depending on how they're powered. The most common is an electric winch driven by a 12-volt motor, but this is limited in performance by the electrical system. Next on the list is a hydraulic winch, powered by a hydraulic pump usually belt driven off the front of the engine. These offer very strong pulling power at low speeds and great

how you are likely to use it. For Challenge competition machines, you need both speed and power, plus the ability to dissipate the considerable heat generated by the motor. By comparison, a car designed for gentle Green Laning only needs a small winch, speed is much less important, and as it won't

controllability, although the system can be a bit heavy. Finally, there are mechanical winches directly driven off the engine, usually in the form of a capstan winch you wrap a rope round. These are very powerful but need skill to operate and are usually quite heavy.

Modern electric winches are very good, and by far the most popular choice. They also usually have a remote switch so you can operate the winch whilst standing next to the car

The wiring has to cope with very high currents, often more than the engine's starter motor, which is a lot. The winch needs a heavy-duty relay, sometimes called a contactor or solenoid, which not only switches the motor on or off but also changes its direction. Cables and connectors must be able to cope with the worst case loading: cables get hot with heavy currents and, as it's likely they will also get covered in mud, they need to be specified to a higher capacity. So if the motor is rated at 300 amps, the cables should be rated at 400 amps. The winch can take a much greater current than the alternator can generate, so the battery takes the brunt of the load. If the winch is small and only to be used for short periods then the cars standard battery may be able to cope. For most installations, though, it's best to install a second battery and a split charge system just for the winch.

All winches should have a free wheel function so you can pull the rope out easily. The rope needs to be guided into the winch roller without rubbing on parts of the winch housing or bumper, so a 'Fairlead' is usually used. This can be a solid lump of metal or hard plastic with curved sides that allows the rope to slide easily, or it can have a set of four rollers.

The rope itself is obviously a vital component, and there's more to it

than meets the eye. Historically, wire rope made from many strands of steel wire was used. Whilst this can be very strong, withstanding being dragged across rough surfaces like rocks, it has limited flexibility so you have to be careful to avoid kinking it on obstacles. It can corrode, so it needs to be cleaned and lubricated after use, and it's also quite heavy, making hauling it up a muddy bank quite hard work. Possibly its biggest snag, though, is that if it breaks under load it becomes quite deadly, and can whip round and cut through flesh with horrific results. To avoid this scenario, you can get heavy blankets that are draped over the middle of the rope before putting it under load. If it snaps then some of the recoil will be damped down, but the main way of avoiding injury is to ensure that no one is standing anywhere near the possible arc of the rope. Steel ropes can fray and the resulting wire ends are very sharp, so it's vital to use very sturdy work gloves when handling steel rope.

The other option is to use a synthetic rope, usually based on Kevlar aramid fibres, with trade names such as Plasma. This has some very big advantages: it's very light, which makes handling it very easy; if it breaks it just drops safely to the floor with no risk of severed limbs; also if it breaks it can be spliced back together very easily

Don't use cheap ropes, such as nylon or hemp, as they're simply not up to the job and a breakage can result in a very bad accident. The downside to synthetic rope is its high price, and also that many winches use the drum as a way of dissipating heat from the motor. This means that if the winch is used a lot a synthetic rope may melt on the drum.

The winch power needed depends on how you will used it, and how stuck you will get! If you are on a slippery surface and just need a winch to get

going, then maybe something as small as a 1000lb winch will do just fine. If you are stuck up to the axles with fallen tree trunks in front of the wheels then you are going to need a lot more, maybe ten times as much pulling power.

The other thing to bear in mind is duty cycle, that is how long and how often the winch will be used. Many cheaper winches save cost by using cheaper bearings and electrical parts. This is fine for occasional use but on something like a Challenge car, where the winch is used repeatedly under high load, you need the highest durability components.

Magazines regularly do winch reviews, and as the technology changes it's worth checking to see what the latest models can offer.

The winch has to be mounted to something solid enough to transmit all that pulling force into the chassis. The best method is usually to use a specially made winch bumper, although winches have been hidden behind panels and mounted onto crossmembers. Winch bumpers use the same mounting points as the standard bumper, so it's absolutely vital that these points are in very good condition.

As well as fitting a winch, you will need some accessories to get the best use from it; things like tree strops, ground anchors, shackles, and pulley blocks. All need a secure home when not in use, so it's worth factoring in a kit locker when you plan a winch installation. Because the kit's quite heavy, the storage box must be strong and held securely so it can't cause an injury in an accident. The safest option is to install a dedicated storage box, bolted securely to the car's structure.

Kinetic energy ropes have a bad reputation, with good reason. Basically, it's a long rope with a small amount of elasticity in. The stuck car is recovered

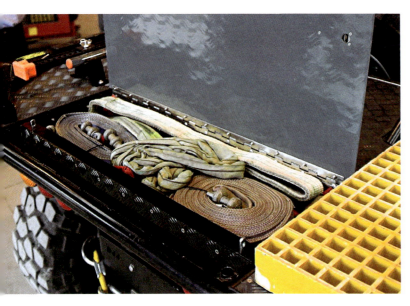

Essential secure kit storage at the back of this competition tray-back; tree strops, shackles, and extensions are all useful. (Courtesy Devon 4x4)

If a log or ditch has stopped the car then a high lift jack might recover the situation. This one is secured to the spare wheel carrier. Note the jacking holes in the heavy-duty bumper.

Replacing the standard lashing eyes with Jate rings provides useful recovery points on a standard car.

Bridging ladders or 'waffle' boards will give a wheel traction in mud, sand, or when crossing a ditch. (Courtesy Devon 4x4)

to be strong enough to cope with such high forces, and all too often they're not. There are many stories of rear bumpers or complete crossmembers being ripped off and flying through the window of the other car. Before employing kinetic energy rope, ensure that both cars are up to the job, and, equally important, that everyone involved in the recovery is properly and professionally trained. Better still, don't use it.

Even if you don't have a winch, if you need to be recovered you have to have something sturdy on the car to attach the rope to. The trouble is that standard bumpers are a bit weak, apart from the rear Defender item, so suitable towing points need to be securely attached to the car.

One way is to fit heavy-duty bumpers with integrated recovery points. Another option is to fit specialist rings to the chassis rails, such as Jate

from its sunken location by a recovery car that's hitched onto the rope and drives off. As the slack is taken up, the rope stretches and stores kinetic energy. When the rope is fully stretched, the recovery car may come to a halt, but the rope is now exerting a very high force on the stuck car. In fact, the force is many times higher than the force that could be transmitted down an ordinary tow rope, and this is where the problem is. The towing points on both cars need

rings. The advantage is that they put the force of recovery straight into the chassis; the disadvantage is that they're positioned slightly under the car so can

A fully-equipped tray-back with central winch, ground anchor (left), and waffle boards. (Courtesy Devon 4x4)

be difficult to access if you have just sunk in mud.

Never use the standard lashing points on the chassis for recovery, these are designed for tying the car down in transport and are nowhere near strong enough for the huge forces involved in recovering a stuck car.

BODY MODS
Pick up

This is quite an appealing conversion that makes the car more useful for carrying big loads at the expense of seating, and of course the load gets wet when it rains.

The Defender was offered as a pick up as standard, and because the body panels bolt together it's fairly straightforward to convert any other body style to a pick up. With Range Rover and Discovery models it's a bit more complicated. The basic principle is that the roof is cut behind the B-pillar line, the rear doors are stripped and welded shut on four-door models, then the remaining pillars are cut off. Before cutting starts, the headlining is removed and the main wiring loom is detached from the roof rails and relocated in the side body. On Range Rovers the lower tailgate can be retained, but on Discoveries the tailgate can be cut down and refitted with an extra hinge at the top to replace the upper one that has been cut off, or it can be replaced with an ally sheet. The sides of the body need to be finished with a capping piece. The load bed has a tendency to fill with rain water so drain holes are need in the floor.

Bobtail

If you are less worried about load capacity there's the 'bobtail' option, where you shorten the boot area leaving virtually no rear overhang. The most popular car for this treatment is the Range Rover. Although it has been done to many Discoveries and the occasional Defender 110, the D90 already has minimal overhang.

The first step on a Range Rover Classic (RRC) is to strip the interior from the back (including the whole headlining). Then the upper and lower tailgate is removed and the roof is unbolted. Next out is the boot floor, which unbolts on most models, and the rear wing panels are removed. Then the fuel tank comes out. Now it gets serious as the rear of the chassis is cut off just behind the rear axle. The body is cut just in front of the rear pillars and about 440mm of the remaining bodywork is removed before the rear pillar section is reattached. A similar cut is made to shorten the alloy roof and rear wings, which are then joined back together by progressively forming small flanges that are riveted and bonded.

At this point the rear side window frames can be cut down to size. The glass can be custom-made to fit, polycarbonate sheeting cut to size, or the aperture could be plated over with ally sheet.

The chassis is completed by welding in box section extensions

A pick up is much more useful than an estate down on the farm; this Discovery is partway through a conversion.

The classic bobtail Range Rover; less overhang means better off-road capability for this competition machine. (Courtesy Devon 4x4)

3. The rear section is welded back in place after trimming to fit the wheelarches. (Courtesy Devon 4x4)

1. First stage is to strip out the interior, tailgate, boot floor, and roof. (Courtesy Devon 4x4)

4. Above: Taking shape: now the roof can be cut and joined with a riveted or bonded strip, and bolted back on. (Courtesy Devon 4x4)

2. After marking up, the rear section is removed and the unwanted metal thrown away. (Courtesy Devon 4x4)

rearwards and making a rear bumper, possibly including a winch, and incorporating bracketry for a small fuel tank.

Then it's just a matter of putting it all back together again; lights, tailgate, and a trimmed boot floor.

Doing this to a Discovery is slightly more complicated as the roof is steel and welded-on, as is the boot floor, but the same principle holds. The main difference is that the rear door

**5. The rear wing just needs trimming at its rear edge so it can rejoin the rear corner piece.
(Courtesy Devon 4x4)**

aperture is removed whole, the unwanted body cut off and then the aperture is reattached.

But if that's still too much bodywork for you, most of the rear body could be removed entirely to make a 'tray-back,' as used in the Australian Outback Challenge trucks by Devon 4x4. This time the body is cut just behind the B-pillar. Defenders can use the rear cab panel from the chassis cab variant, Range Rovers and Discoveries can either be finished with a fabricated panel or fit an aftermarket moulded cab back.

The chassis is trimmed and finished in the same way as the bobtail but with a fabricated frame built on top. This gives a flat deck that extends the full width of the car. For an example see chapter 9.

For an unusual convertible, the roof on Range Rover and Defender models unbolts. This also makes it easier to fit internal roll cages. For competition use the cage must attach to the chassis and so goes through the floor just behind the front seats, usually the body is then hard mounted to the chassis to simplify things.

A tray-back in action: zero overhang and easy access to recovery kit is ideal for this Challenge truck. (Courtesy Devon 4x4)

Middle left: The point of no return: everything behind the spring hanger is removed. (Courtesy Devon 4x4)

Middle right: For a competition vehicle, at this stage the mounting turret for the roll cage is welded onto the chassis. (Courtesy Devon 4x4)

Bottom left: A new rear crossmember finishes off the rear chassis. This D44 type houses a winch, and has recovery points, too. For a longer wheelbase, the radius arms and top wishbone have been lengthened. (Courtesy Devon 4x4)

Bottom right: The rear tray is fabricated from strong tube on this competition car. (Courtesy Devon 4x4)

With the rear body completely removed, there are a huge number of possibilities for the coil-sprung chassis. (Courtesy Devon 4x4)

The front wings have been fabricated using a strong tube frame and bolt-on flat ally panels, which are strong and easy to replace if damaged.

ELECTRICS

Electrics need to be modified with great care. New circuits must be powered from a new supply; never just cut into an existing supply as that circuit might be overloaded as a result. If you are adding a few new circuits, it's worth fitting a new fuse box to safely supply them all.

Good earths are essential, and sensitive electronics such as gauges or fuel-injection sensors must have a separate earth to high power circuits such as lights or fans, otherwise the delicate signals can be upset by the high currents.

If you are fitting extra electrical systems, make sure the alternator is adequate for the job. It's worth adding up all the loads and working out what the worst case demand will be. Start by writing down the wattage of all the things on the car, then think about which systems might be switched on at the same time for long periods. Don't worry about things such as electric windows that are only used briefly as the battery can assist with brief peak demands. There are also some things that definitely won't be on at the same time, such as main and dipped beam, or cooling fans and demisters, so only one of the two needs to be added in. Usually, the highest load is when starting out on a cold winter's day, with window demisters on, heater blower on full, and the lights on. With all this lot added up you will have a total wattage which represents the worst case for the alternator. To calculate the current in amps, divide the wattage by the alternator voltage, usually about 13.8 to 14.5 volts. Once you have the worst case current, add a safety margin because there's always a chance that something has been forgotten, you may choose to add something later, or because alternators wear and it's best not to run anything at its limit for long periods. So add about 20 per cent to your total current and that's the smallest alternator size that will work reliably on your project.

Some cars may drain the battery when left for long periods due to various small loads such as clock and control units. Some people fit a battery isolator switch that simply disconnects the battery when not needed. Usually, it goes in the negative lead for safety when working near the battery. If the switch is in the engine bay it also doubles as an added security measure, although it obviously defeats any alarm system fitted.

For safety, on a competition car a cut-off switch is wired in that

The relays, fuses and ECU in this Tomcat are mounted away from splashing mud, and laid out in a logical order to make future fault-finding easier.

disconnects the battery and also stops the engine. A simple battery isolator switch would not stop a running engine because the alternator will continue to power the ignition circuit. So the switch not only disconnects the battery but also disconcerts power to the engine ignition circuit. If the engine was spinning fast, this sudden removal of load would cause the alternator to over voltage and blow the regulator

A battery cut-off switch isolates all electrical circuits when not needed, ensuring the battery isn't drained.

For competition cars it's important to keep moisture away from switches, and the danger of being struck, either when kit's thrown in the cab, or by accident when the car is in motion.

For safety reasons in competition use, the ignition steering lock is removed and replaced with a starter button and separate switches for ignition and auxiliary functions.

Fuse blocks lead directly to relay bases on this neat installation in a challenge car; all connections properly sealed and secure. (Courtesy Devon 4x4)

Below left: Self-amalgamating tape is superb at sealing connectors and insulating wires, and can also be used to make grommets.

Below right: Use the right connector for each job; there isn't one that does all so a selection box is essential for big electrical modifications.

circuit up, so the cut-off switch also connects a high power resistor to the alternator to give it some load.

A split charge system has a second battery connected to the alternator via a high power diode. This acts as a one-way valve and means the secondary battery can be charged but not power any of the car's systems.

This battery is used only for the winch or other auxiliary systems and is completely separate from the rest of the vehicle. A current limiting resistor on the alternator connection prevents excessive loading on the alternator and main battery.

When fitting new connectors use good quality crimps, these, as

mentioned, must have a part that grips the insulation of the cable to relieve strain as well as a part that grips the wire. Avoid the clip on connectors, such as 'Scotch-lock,' as these can cut the wires and the connection pressure is usually poor, making them unreliable. Although, to be fair, I have seen a few do a good job as a short-term fix.

Immobilisers

It's an unfortunate fact that these cars are targeted by thieves, either to sell abroad or break down for parts. This makes an immobiliser an essential piece of equipment for any modified Land Rover, and there are a number of very good kits available which cut into vital electrical circuits to render the car unstartable without major rewiring. Usually, the fuel pump, starter, injection system (where fitted), and ignition/stop solenoid are interrupted by a set of hidden relays and the wiring neatly tucked away in the loom.

Shorting the trigger signal to the coil to ground via a resistor makes the system difficult to bypass, as long as the added wires are well hidden.

Using an existing redundant switch to operate a homemade immobiliser.

There's also the simple option of interrupting these circuits with relays operated by a switch hidden somewhere in the cab. Of course, a clued up thief can simply clip on a few extra wires and bypass all this, but there's a cunning way to fox them a little more on petrol cars. The immobiliser relay can be used to short the ignition feed from the contact breakers/trigger module to ground via a small resistor. If a new ignition feed was to be clipped on now, the system still wouldn't work.

Unfortunately, none of this will stop a determined thief who is willing to tow your car away. To make this task more difficult there are devices that jam the brake pedal down, or, to go a step further, 'line lock' valves – used by drag racers to lock the front brakes on whilst doing burn outs – can be fitted to the brake lines in a hidden location.

However, many thefts are by casual opportunists, and one very easy way to fox someone not familiar with Land Rovers is to leave the transfer box in neutral.

TOWING

These Land Rovers make fantastic tow cars, and, luckily, the provision of a towing bracket was though of from the start. Land Rover offer original equipment brackets, as do many other companies, but this hasn't stopped some people fabricating their own systems from inadequate materials. For this reason, check that any towing equipment you buy has a manufacturers mark and is up to the job.

This adjustable height tow hitch not only allows for different trailer ride heights but can also compensate for different tyres used on the Land Rover.

The stays attach to the lashing eye bolts. The chassis in this area and the rear crossmember must be in good condition.

One of the problems is that the top of the bracket mounts onto the rear crossmember, which is a traditional rot trap on all three models, so it's a good idea to inspect this area thoroughly before use. The bracket is stabilised with two links onto the chassis rails. Before fitting a bracket the bolts and chassis mountings should be protected with spray grease or similar.

There are two types of trailer electrical socket: the light coloured one is the '12S' for powering the internal devices in a caravan; the more important one is the black '12N' which runs the lights and indicators.

12N wiring pin designations

Pin	Wire colours	Function
1	Black/White	Left-hand indicator
2	White	Rear fog light
3	Brown	Earth
4	Black/Green	Right-hand indicator
5	Grey/Red	Side lights
6	Black/Red	Stop lights
7	Grey/Black	Side lights

The Discovery has a very handy electrical connector in the load bed fitted as standard that simply plugs into the trailer socket lead, as long as you buy the genuine Land Rover item.

For other models, the electrics will need to be spliced into the rear light wiring. A special indicator module is needed, which most later cars have fitted as standard. Earlier ones will have a trailer indicator light that flashes in sync with the indicators when the trailer is connected, and this needs to be replaced. Luckily, the newer module simply plugs into the same connector.

There are a few peculiarities to Land Rover towing brackets. As the car rides quite high, the bracket can easily end up too high for normal trailers. There are some off-road trailers available that ride equally high, but for most normal purposes the bracket needs some sort of drop plate to put the tow ball

at the right height. Adjustable brackets are available, with a range of holes and a heavy-duty pin arrangement, to allow the height to be set up to suit what ever type of trailer you want.

One problem with a low mounted tow bracket is that in heavy off-road situations it can dig in and act like an anchor. For this reason, there are a range of removable brackets, but even the standard Land Rover bracket can be loosened and swung up out of the way with a small tie up plate – a little more work than a quick-release bracket but a lot cheaper.

Most trailers use the standard ball and socket method of attachment, but there are other possibilities. Military trailers use an eye and jaw arrangement, which is much stronger and the preferred method of towing off-road where the forces on the hitch are much greater. Obviously, the mountings and bracket must be strong enough to match, and may require a thick spreader plate behind the hitch. The most popular is the NATO hitch, which allows the use of military trailers such as the popular Sanky range.

This tank guard incorporates mountings for quick-release towing brackets. The pins are held in place with simple P-clips, and can be removed easily to prevent the guard digging in on heavy off-road work.

Another advantage of a quick-release fitting is that other brackets can be slipped in, such as this recovery point.

LPG

Many V8s have been converted to Liquefied Petroleum Gas (LPG), and, unfortunately, most of them will need some degree of mending due to the highly variable quality of installation. LPG has the potential to halve your fuel bills, but beware: there are many badly set up systems which run very rich, resulting in less saving than expected.

From a performance point of view, only gas-injection is worth considering because the alternative 'mixer ring' venturi restricts airflow dramatically. However, if power isn't your main concern the cheaper and simpler mixer system may be just the job.

LPG has some useful properties. It has a higher octane rating than petrol so modifying the engine to give a higher compression ratio and advancing the ignition can give a gas-injected engine about 10 per cent more power, but it needs a dedicated tune. So for dual petrol/LPG fuel the engine must remain standard to avoid detonation on petrol. However, you can still benefit from a switchable ECU like the Emerald, with an ignition map for each fuel; running more advance on LPG.

LPG being a gas isn't capable of lubricating the valve seats, and this can lead to higher seat wear than normal if the engine is regularly worked hard – although if full throttle is rarely used, this may not be a problem. It's possible to fit an additional oiling system such as Flashlube, although getting it to distribute evenly to all cylinders can be difficult.

Finding space for the gas tanks is always tricky. LPG tanks have to be very rugged to cope with high pressures and survive in a heavy crash. Inside the tank there's a gas volume above the liquid fuel, so a 100-litre tank will actually only hold 80 litres of liquid fuel. Most dual fuel conversions see about a 10 per cent drop on mpg with gas, so a 100-litre working capacity LPG tank should give a similar range to a standard 90-litre petrol tank. The simple option is to fit a large cylinder tank in the boot space, but this takes up most of the load area and renders folding rear seats a bit pointless. A common solution is to fit two small tanks between the chassis and sills, one on each side. On a 100in chassis a 35-litre tank is the largest that can fit here, so between the two of them that's a total of 70 litres with a usable capacity of 56 litres. Some people add a third small tank; in the boot space where the spare wheel goes on a Range Rover or one of the rear stowage bins on a Discovery, Defenders have the void behind the wheelarches. Another option is to fit two cylinders in place of the petrol tank, and fit a smaller tank in the

A good conversion; all the wires and hoses are neatly routed and all connections professionally finished.

Individual solenoid gas injectors are fitted in 'sequential' systems. The gas ECU converts the petrol injection pulses into equivalent gas injector pulses.

When fitting the tanks and filler point, consideration should be given to what might happen in a collision.

heavier than air so any leak will pool in the lowest area. During installation and testing garages with pits should be avoided, as should parking near drains. Any leak inside the car could be disastrous, so tanks have to have a leak proof box fitted round the valve gear with a generous vent pipe leading straight to the underside of the car. To help detect leaks a stenching agent is added to the gas during processing, so if you can smell gas from a converted car, other than when it's being refuelled, there's a fault which must be repaired immediately.

LPG is a very good fuel, and when set up correctly can make the engine run smoother and more economically. In years to come, with increasing oil prices, this fuel makes a lot of sense for old Land Rover Petrol engines.

rear wing area – obviously not the safest place for a petrol tank if the car is in a crash. In contrast, LPG tanks have been known to survive being hit by a high speed train – they're quite solid!

Because LPG is stored under high pressure – from about 5bar up to 25bar depending on temperature – it's easy for a small leak to be very serious. LPG is

ELECTRIC DRIVE

Back in the '70s a number of companies experimented with electric Range Rovers, coupling a modest drive motor to the transfer box and filling the engine bay with lead acid batteries. Needless to say, it wasn't a commercial success.

But now we have a number of high power drive motors and compact battery systems. For instance, the Mini E has a 150kW motor which if fitted into one of these Land Rovers would give performance superior to a 3.5 V8.

With oil prices set to rise steadily it's only a matter of time before such conversions become readily available.

Chapter 9
Conversions

For some people, the three body styles offered by Land Rover are not quite what they want. The basic chassis and running gear make a superb base for a completely new vehicle and there are many fine companies offering complete vehicle conversions, here are just a few.

TOMCAT

The idea was simple, take only the parts you actually need from a Range Rover or Discovery to get from A to B, if a part doesn't contribute to going faster then its removed. It's a theory that has created some of the greatest race cars of history, such as the Lotus 7.

The Tomcat conversion starts with either a Range Rover or Discovery rolling chassis. Every part is removed, the chassis cleaned, and the various outriggers and brackets removed. The Tomcat is available in a range of wheelbases; long for high speed stability and short for low speed manoeuvrability. Many Comp Safari racers favour the standard 100in wheelbase, but for other wheelbases the chassis is split in the middle and rebuilt to the desired size.

As well as removing unnecessary brackets, the chassis has its rear overhang removed and a Defender rear crossmember welded-in. The front also gets trimmed back to the front crossmember, and short Defender-style bumper mounts are formed.

At this stage, there are a number of suspension options available. For fast competition, many racers convert the rear axle to use the same radius arms as the front suspension, with a Panhard rod to control sideways movement. This is basically the same type of system the Discovery 2 used as standard.

Damper mounts can be changed for ultra-strong items made from tube, which can be made specifically for racing long-travel dampers. It's quite common for a Tomcat to have 12in of wheel travel, which not only allows for greater axle articulation but also makes a big improvement to how the car lands and remains stable after big jumps.

Another Tomcat option is to move the engine mounts back about 12in which balances the car for high speed work. For low speed steep hill climbs leaving the engine forward can help

A tomcat at speed turning into a chicane on gravel; long wheelbase options enhance high speed stability.

The full body option for less drag at speed; vents at the rear let hot air escape from the rear-mounted radiator.

Dry race visibility is helped by removing the quick-release doors.

Fording is usually done slowly, but on a Comp Safari there's no time to waste. (Courtesy Chris Nunn)

Relatively lightweight and long travel suspension allows the Tomcat to tackle rough ground at high speed.

keep the front wheels on the ground. If the mounts are moved back by the recommended distance then the front and rear propshafts can be swapped over, avoiding the need for custom units.

The main part of the conversion is the racing specification space frame roll cage welded directly to the chassis. This makes a very strong structure that can take the hammering of extreme competition whilst still being very light.

The bodywork consists of fibreglass outer panels and aluminium sheet for the cab floor and bulkheads.

This is why they have snorkels! On these types of races the doors are kept on.

It's available in a number of styles from a minimal bonnet and wings right up to a full Dakar-style covering including streamlined rear body, doors, and roof. It's amazingly light, even the full body systems only weigh about 50kg. Depending on the specification these race cars can weigh as little as 1300kg.

Weight distribution makes a huge difference to how the machine behaves when driven on the limit. Comp Safari racers often get airborne over big jumps so things like the radiator and battery are moved to the back of the cab to aid landing. Other sports, such as Challenge, need the weight forward. All these arrangements are possible on this type of machine because the owner can fit components where ever they like, tailoring it to their own preference and driving style.

For this reason, no two Tomcats are the same. Each has its own story to tell and shows a different approach to tackling the problems that extreme competition provides.

DAKAR AND BUSH RANGER

This is another space frame conversion with fibreglass bodywork, but, where the Tomcat preserves the classic Defender look, the Dakar presents an altogether more striking image based on the Range Rover/ Discovery platform.

The main focus of the original design was fun, but the performance potential of a lightweight (often about 1500kg) all-terrain vehicle were soon recognised and examples have

This special Dakar was created for a BBC TV show, featuring two front ends joined back-to-back and a massive roll cage.

The Dakar used the donor car to a large extent, including chassis, suspension, and drive train, and it could even take the dash and climate control.

The distinctive front end. Most road cars have the lights bolted to the bull bar.

been raced in all branches of off-road motorsport. Most Dakars are used as road cars and Play Day toys. There's a greater focus on comfort than on a thoroughbred race car and the kit retains the original Land Rover front floor and bulkhead. This means that luxuries like a heater and air-conditioning are possibilities, together with electric Range Rover leather seats, the whole dash assembly, and stowage bins – there's even provision for rear seats.

The body style was first seen on the 2wd Cortina-based Rotrax kit car, but putting it on a custom frame mounted to a Range Rover rolling chassis gave it the capability its looks promised. The overall package can be customised hugely by the owner, making every car very personal, which is probably why there's such a strong owners club.

It has also spawned an Australian version called the Bushranger, which is slightly longer and has many detail differences. Bushrangers have proved very popular, and there was even a military version.

The appeal of this design is in its striking looks – like something out of a SciFi film, it generates interest where ever it goes. On road the reduced weight improves performance and can make the handling feel sharper, depending on what sort of springs and ride height is chosen. Off-road the Range Rover capabilities are enhanced by the drastically reduced rear overhang. The high wheelarches allow for very large tyres to be fitted, in fact, the design needs large tyres to look 'right.'

Driving with the optional doors off provides a superb view of the road on the drivers side, making placing the vehicle on tricky off-road courses much easier. For wet weather, a canvas roof can be added and there are options of two or four doors made from lightweight GRP.

The bull bar is a prominent and distinctive feature, and not just cosmetic as it includes mountings for the lights and indicators.

This machine is great fun, with some degree of every day practicality as well as competition potential, unlike the other two vehicles featured in this chapter which are firmly targeted at competition.

D44 OUTBACK CHALLENGE

Unlike the previous examples, this conversion remains the car it started out as, just with every component modified in some way to transform the vehicle's capability.

These conversions are built for a single-minded purpose – to win. Challenge events take on the most gruelling terrain the planet can throw at them. (Courtesy Devon 4x4)

Challenge events are run across the world. Based on standard models, the cars have to negotiates cliffs, rivers, boulders, and winch themselves out of near impossible situations.

Devon 4x4 have been winning trophies with their Range Rover and Defender-based trucks in this ultimate test of man and machine for many years. The principle is to use the Land Rover's inherent strengths and completely re-engineer its weaknesses.

Although it still looks like a Defender the car is completely re-engineered. (Courtesy Devon 4x4)

The distinctive tray-back allows quick access to the recovery gear, and the lack of rear overhang – coupled with the extreme suspension – makes it all but unstoppable. (Courtesy Devon 4x4)

The key element to the conversion is the fabricated rear chassis that incorporates winch mounting and recovery points.
(Courtesy Devon 4x4)

To this end, Land Rover axles are used, but with a tough bolt-on alloy diff cover, with new trick diffs, stronger half shafts, and modifications to stop the crown wheel being pushed out of line.

A good quality standard engine is used, but with competition exhaust and intake. The intake incorporates a snorkel which has a performance filter at the top. The custom exhaust terminates just in front of the new rear crossmember, minimising the chance of it being crushed as the car slides off rocks.

The most obvious change is the tray-back, which is a completely new structure fabricated onto the chassis. The rear chassis is a completely new fabrication and is joined to the original chassis at the rear spring mounts, which shortens and strengthens the chassis, and also incorporates a very strong winch mount.

Unlike the first two examples in this chapter, these cars wear their roll cage on the outside of the bodywork. Rolling at low speed is an ever present risk so it makes sense for the cage to protect the bodywork as well as the occupants.

Tube work is also used to make a frame that replaces the front wings. Aluminium sheet is used to fill the gaps and makes the front end very tough, yet relatively easy to fix when it gets scraped and bashed in the heat of competition.

The suspension is engineered for very high travel. The rear featured dislocateable springs and relocation cones coupled with double dampers to share the load. All the joints are redesigned to allow them to move through the much larger angles competition axles can move through.

SPECIALS

There have been many specialist conversions over the years, too. A very small number of cars have been made for working with birds of prey, featuring a central rear seat that can be raised to get a better view of the bird in action.

For many years, most small airports featured a Range Rover-based 6x4 fire tender, which needed the extra axle to carry several tons of water and foaming agent.

Crossing very boggy land has always fired the imagination of inventors, and there have been a few conversions replacing the wheels with tracks, such as the Cuthbertson conversion which bolts on to the standard hubs.

A more radical conversion was the Land Rover Centaur half track, which used a shortened track system from a Scorpion armoured vehicle.

So, it seems no matter what the challenge someone will make a Land Rover to tackle it.

Land Rovers are excellent 'go anywhere' vehicles, but boggy ground needs very low ground pressure from wide flat tracks. (Courtesy Land Rover)

These conversions use the original axles and suspension, replacing the road wheel with a sprocket that the whole track system pivots off. (Courtesy Land Rover)

All three coil-sprung variants have been converted to six-wheel fire tenders at some point, and many older vehicles are still in service in small airfields today. (Courtesy Land Rover)

www.velocebooks.com / www.veloce.co.uk
All current books • New book news • Special offers • Gift vouchers

Chapter 10
Case studies

After having gone through so may options for modifying these magnificent cars, lets see how some enthusiasts have put it all together to make some very capable and fun machines.

The cars I have chosen are ones built by enthusiasts. I wanted to show what ordinary people can achieve in the real world. There are many more extreme machines built by professional engineering companies and racers, but they're already well-documented on their own websites, and quite often the level of modification is out of reach and not really relevant to the average enthusiast.

Of course, these cars are very personal. Far more than just a list of parts on a spec sheet, every one has a story to tell about the problems the owner has tackled and the decisions they made, and ultimately the enjoyment they were rewarded with.

RANGE ROVER CLASSIC VOGUE SE 3.9 V8

This is the most extreme car in this chapter, yet it manages to look amazingly understated, which is quite deliberate and took a lot of thought by owner/builder Franc Buxton. The car had to remain an every day usable car because it's used for commuting and the annual family camping trip,

but Frank also enjoys Green Laning and the occasional Play Day. He has an unstoppable curiosity which often results in conversations starting with 'I wonder if I can do that ...'

To avoid it turning into one of those 'long-term projects' Franc set himself a tight deadline – in just 8 months the car was booked to go on the club Green Lane weekend. Passengers were relying on him and accommodation was booked and paid for, so it had to be done on time, no matter what.

The engine is the utterly splendid Jaguar/Land Rover

It looks almost standard, but the bonnet bulge, discreet winch below the number plate, and supercharger whine are all clues.

Further clues are the jackable sills, neatly hidden underslung LPG tanks, side-mounted bonnet Aerocatches, and heavy-duty bumpers.

The heart of the beast; a 4.2-litre supercharged Jaguar V8 capable of over 400bhp on gas, mated to a P38a ZF autobox. (Courtesy F Buxton)

engine with an adaptor plate he cut from a 'ruddy great big slab of ally,' and the torque converter is mounted on a modified Jag flex plate.

You'll probably not be surprised to hear that a Jag engine doesn't 'bolt straight in' to an RRC.

Not only did the chassis need modifying to fit the engine mounts further back, the exhausts point backwards so a large chunk of bulkhead had to be removed. To clear the front of the engine, a RR P38A steering box was mounted on the outside of the chassis.

This required completely new Panhard and steering rods, which cleverly minimise bump steer and are significantly stronger than standard.

Cutting through the bodywork revealed a significant amount of hidden corrosion. Feverish activity ensued with many of Franc's chums helping out, and lets face it; no project built in a shed has ever succeeded without a bunch of friends to help out.

Whilst some removable panels were fabricated from aluminium, the important bits, including footwells, floor, and inner wings, were repaired in sheet steel, making a much stronger shell and a nice snug fit round the new power plant.

Franc removed the front road springs so the axle sat hard on the bump stops. This meant various parts, such as the steering damper, trackrod, and diff casing, contacted the sump, so off they came to have large chunks removed and new aluminium welded-on.

He also found that the bonnet didn't quite clear the supercharger, hence the subtle bulge which rather complements the otherwise remarkably standard looking car – if you look closely you will also spot the cunning side-mounted Aerocatch bonnet pins.

The cooling system is a work of art. Based on a RRC radiator with electric

supercharged 4.2-litre V8, as used in the Range Rover Sport. The original ZF 4HP22 can struggle with very high torque so the stronger 4HP24E off a Range Rover P38A was drafted into service. This was mated to the Jag

It's a brave man that cuts up his family car in order to build a dream. Here, the bulkhead is trimmed to fit the engine. (Courtesy F Buxton)

A full engine bay; supercharger, LPG system, split charge, winch controls, and ARB air pump all sit neatly together.

Engine ancillaries dictated that the steering box had to move outboard of the chassis. The solution is a P38a box and custom link rods.

fans, it also has a custom-built radiator for the air to water intercoolers with its own electric coolant pump.

All the associated wiring had to be stripped out and remade to incorporate the Jaguar electronic throttle and the engine control system.

The Sport exhaust manifolds were attached to a custom system made from a mixture of Land Rover parts cut-and-shut to fit.

At that point everyone was called round for a ceremonial start up, and the engine fired up first time, sounding utterly awesome in the small garage.

As this was the main family car it had to be economical, so Franc fitted a top of the range LPG system with full sequential injection. It has two underslung tanks (with recesses in the floor for good ground clearance) plus one in the boot – range is important for the annual family holiday as well as several Green Laning trips each year.

The car has several subtle but effective off-road modifications like protection plates, jackable sills, and the heavy-duty solid steel bumpers incorporating recovery points. Have a good look at the photos and you might just spot the front winch which is brilliantly subtle. The usual boot contents include a high lift jack, felling axe, and a bow saw (all of which

get used) so the car's total weight is approaching that of the Range Rover Sport.

As mentioned earlier, the auto 'box was not quite normal. Franc built his own gearbox ECU and now has full manual shift control commanded from a steering column switch, as well as an auto option with his own shift program.

The handling has been developed over time by Franc and is supple without being too soft. The front springs are off the back end of a Defender, and the rear ones are police spec RRC with 40mm spacers. Dampers are adjustable Konis all round and poly bushes keep the links under control. He also fitted Discovery anti-roll bars, which can be detached for extreme off-road use.

The inside bristles with technology. As well as the usual GPS and CB mounts, there's also a special platform for the laptop computer – useful for navigating, and for tuning the engine and gearbox ECUs.

ARB diff lock control switches sit next to an appropriate message from Franc's daughter.

Sheer driving pleasure, and the satisfaction of a job well done.

There's a very neat LED indicator to show which gear is engaged, and this also displays the status of the gearbox in case of any problems.

The ARB air operated diff lock switches are neatly incorporated in the centre console, and there's a set of switches to the right of the steering column to allow the idle speed to be raised for heavy winching.

The winch has a synthetic 'Plasma' rope which is stronger than steel and weighs almost nothing. The winch is powered from a split charge system with twin Optima batteries.

The car was finished just in time for the planned Laning trip, although, on the way to the event, fate threw another stinger in the path of progress when one of the rear drive shafts (or mechanical fuses!) snapped.

With not enough time for a repair, Franc simply engaged the rear ARB diff lock, removed the remains of the shaft and carried on – determined to enjoy his amazing creation on its first proper trip out. Remarkably, it completed the weekend in Wales (including Strata Florida) with only three-wheel drive perfectly – much to the relief of the passengers.

Since then, all the little jobs around the car have been finished and it's putting in sterling service as a reliable, comfortable, practical, go anywhere machine that just happens to be rather swift.

Top mods
• Jaguar/LandRover 4.2 V8 Supercharged with owner-calibrated ECU.
• Owner-built exhaust system.
• LPG sequential injection system, 3 tanks 400bhp on gas.
• ZF4HP24EH auto gearbox with 'Tiptronic'-style manual mode, owner-built gearbox ECU.
• ARB air operated diff locks front and rear.
• Uprated springs and dampers.
• P38 steering box.
• Anti-roll bars.
• Pollybushes.
• LR Alloy wheels with Kumho Road Venture tyres.

Chassis mods include:
• Heavy-duty rear bumper.
• Dixon Bate tow jaw.
• Heavy-duty front bumper, incorporating a winch, movable tow bracket, underbody protection plates and Aerocatch bonnet pins.
• Ally chequer plate protectors.
• Custom security device.
• Custom lap top stand.
• Integrated GPS aerial.
• Custom load cover with integrated HiLift jack mount, CB, integrated mains supply, and split charge twin battery system.

DEFENDER 110 WAGON 300TDI
There are many wild, and even mad conversions out there, but this one stands out because every modification serves a purpose that is utterly focused on how the car is going to be used.

Nick gets an amazing amount of use out of this car and it has now done over 220 thousand hard miles under his ownership. He marshals at Comp Safari events all over the UK, having to reach some fairly inaccessible locations and set up base for a weekend. He also does continental expeditions through Europe, clocking up huge mileages on both rough tracks and at speed on Motorways, as well as tackling the more challenging Green Lanes that his off-road club ventures on. To top it all,

A hard worked Defender; snorkel, jackable sills, and front protection bars all get regularly tested – the bumper is evidence of hard use.

Standard looks are, once again, deceptive: diff guards, steering guards, and uprated links make this one tough Land Rover.

this car is also his every day commuter, tackling a mix of city driving and fast A roads.

So what he needed was a car that was fast, economical, has a large load area, handles well at speed on road, and wont get stuck off-road either – quite a tall order!

With the need to improve performance without ruining economy, engine modification focused on reliability and was limited to just reversing the boost capsule to reduce turbo lag.

The suspension is very well thought through: the springs are relatively stiff and the damping firm so there's remarkably little roll on corners and the road manners are very good. To increase off-road articulation, the rear axle has a dislocation system; so although the front axle is held fairly stiffly, the rear axle can drop into deep ruts and all four wheels stay in contact with the ground. This make the car very capable on the sorts of terrain it was built for. The axles are protected from rocks with diff protectors and a steering

The battle-scarred sills tell the tale of many adventures.

Trick suspension with dual rate springs, performance dampers, and tubular damper mounts.

guard – nothing excessive, just enough to do the job properly.

Tyre choice is critical for this combination to work. After years of using AT tyres, Nick switched to Kumho KL74 tyres. Both types feature very course tread blocks that are quite stiff on the tyre body. This means the tyres

don't wobble about, get hot on the road at speed, or waste engine power, so the wear rate is also lower.

He needed enough storage for all the camping equipment necessary for long weekends away, plus all the safety and communications equipment used when marshalling. The stowage system

Proof of use; the official plate of a competition support vehicle. Such volunteers are essential in motorsport.

Interior conversion includes stowage for camping gear and recovery equipment.

Says it all ...

has evolved over the years, and now incorporates a plywood liner in the rear with stowage nets on the sides. There's a removable flat floor running between the rear wheelarches, with stowage bins underneath that can be pulled out from the rear. The flat floor allows a camping bed to go in so Nick has the option of sleeping in the car if the conditions preclude a tent. The lining not only provides a base for the stowage system but also insulates the car to make camping more pleasant.

Often bulky items are fixed to the roof, so a series of small U-bolts normally used for attaching exhausts are fixed to the gutters to allow very secure tethering of roof loads. These also support a canvas roof when setting up a camp; providing a dry and shady spot for the table, chairs, and mobile cooker – very civilised.

Top mods

• Custom dual rate springs: 1in lift and 20 per cent stiffer. The top coils are a lower rate and are normally compressed fully. When the wheel drops significantly these uncoil and act as a soft extra spring for increased wheel travel.

• DeCarbon long travel dampers all round: the fronts are mounted into tubular damper top mounts 2in shorter than standard to allow for greater axle drop.

• QT drilled front radius arms cranked 3 degrees to compensate for the extra lift. Cranked rear radius arms to allow full articulation. The increased ride height causes the differential drive flange and front propshafts to wear excessively fast so a double Cardon unit custom-made by Dave Mac Propshafts was fitted, which has proven very reliable.

• Equipe polyurethane suspension bushes throughout, mid firmness. So far they have covered over 120 thousand miles without significant wear.

• Scorpion Racing steel steering guard. The steering bars at the front of the axle are thicker and protected by a standard Land Rover tubular front guard.

• South Down 4x4 jackable heavy-duty sills.

• Swing-away spare wheel carrier.

• Heavy-duty tow hitch with a demountable tow ball on a substantial fuel tank guard.

• Mantek snorkel which, despite having been battered by a great many trees,

The roof brackets provide anchor points for the canvas roof when setting up camp at a race event.

and branches is still going strong. At the top is a cap that prevents rain water filling the tube. Inside the sealed filter housing is an ITG sponge performance air filter, which can be washed out when it starts to get full.

• The fuel pump boost capsule has been turned 180 degrees and refitted to make a marked improvement in acceleration without effecting cruising fuel economy.

• Mangles Modular steel wheels wearing Kumho KL74 265/75/16 MT tyres.

• Hella 7 inch headlights.

• CB rig with a wing top mounted aerial.

• The load bed has a flexible load retaining system: tie down points can be simply added where they're needed.

• Load area modified to have flat base with storage bins underneath. Stowage on side panels and U-bolt load hooks on gutters.

When snow prevents most people from driving, John starts smiling and fires up the Discovery. (Courtesy J Wilby)

DISCOVERY 300TDI

The focus of this project is fun. John needed something to lighten the mood after a serious illness, and this certainly fits the bill. It's mainly used for Green Lanes and Play Days, "I have been into Green Laning for the last 7 years and have owed an assortment of Land Rovers in that time, ranging from a series III 2.5-litre diesel to a Range Rover Classic with 4.2-litre V8. When my last Discovery 200Tdi succumbed to rot in some very awkward places I decided that I needed to buy another and swap all my off-road parts over, as that was the cheapest way forward."

John found a late model 300Tdi XS with some signs of repair work to the rear of the chassis and a small hole in the drivers side outer sill, but otherwise in good order.

This car is built for fun; clear evidence of fun is dripping from every part of it here. (Courtesy J Wilby)

The first thing was to fit the 2in body lift. John comments, "I prefer lifting them this way rather than a suspension lift because it doesn't alter the steering geometry."

Undoing the body mounts and ties went well, except for one at the back that had to be ground off. However, but as is often the case, striping the car revealed more work – in this case a rusted out rear chassis mount that had to be replaced.

With the body set up it was time to turn to the bumpers. John wanted a sturdy setup that could take the knocks of Play Day fun, so a padded A-bar and a good chin spoiler that came with the car were sold to raise funds for the modifications – John already had a pair of bumpers on the 200 ready to swap over. "The front bumper was a heavy-duty winch bumper that had a Defender A bar welded-on it. At the same time, I had a Range Rover Classic steering guard that had to be put in place first, as everything was a little tight for space where the bumper bolts go." In addition, a rusty bull bar off a 300 donated light protectors which were welded in place.

Unfortunately, as the rear bumper came off a 200 it did not have provision for rear lights, so some remedial work was needed. "I got a set of Defender rear lights and a set of guards and fitted them. I also had a detachable tow bar that fits nice and snug against the chassis and offers a better alternative than the original tow bar, which pretty much acted as a plough".

To further add to the protection, a pair of diff guards were slipped on, and attention turned to the vulnerable sills. John points out that "sill mounted guards are a preferable option due to the body lift. If I had gone for chassis mounted items there would be a 2in gap." Taking off the plastic sill trim revealed some hidden rot which had to be welded up first – a common problem.

The next addition was the full length roof rack. "It can be a bind when Green Laning and you have a lot of overhanging trees, but I needed the roof rack for when I transported the family camping equipment. I also fitted a light bar and all the spotlights."

Extreme suspension travel and big tyres maintain traction. (Courtesy J Wilby)

With all the extra weight bearing down on the rear John noticed the rear springs were sagging, so fitted 2in spacers to get it to sit level again.

The plan was to fit much bigger 33in tyres, so the wheelarches needed cutting away, "It's scary stuff taking the angle grinder to the bodywork but its got to be done."

Not happy with the car's suspension, John decided it needed further modification in the form of a Llama 4x4 extreme suspension kit. This consisted of heavy-duty springs, long travel dampers, and relocating cones. To cope with the greater articulation, John fitted 5in braided brake hoses.

As the car was expected to spend a fair amount of time in water, all the carpets and sound deadening material was removed to prevent it holding water. John planned to use the 200 snorkel but it didn't fit the 300 air box so a new one was purchased. The visco fan was removed and electric fans fitted.

Then attention turned to the exhaust. John cut off the rear box and rebuilt the system to exit out the side, so it was less vulnerable.

"I now had a pretty well spec'd Green Lane machine that could handle most things thrown at it. The whole point of doing these mods is to use it, so most weekends you will find me on a Green Lane somewhere in the country. Despite the fact that I can go down lanes that lesser spec'd vehicles would find challenging, that isn't the point of Green Laning for me.

The lifted body improves tyre clearance, but if it does get stuck then the winch will save the day. (Courtesy J Wilby)

The flattest, most unchallenging Green Lanes still hold an appeal. It's about getting the family out and enjoying our countryside. We are not able to walk huge amounts because I have a medical condition and our daughter has weak joints because of Downs Syndrome. We normally go out in a group of vehicles (usually about 3 or 4 to a group). There is nothing better than parking up on a mountainside and watching Red Kites in Wales with a nice cup of tea."

Top mods
- Cooper STT 33x12.50x15 on 15in black steel rims.
- Plastic wheelarch extensions.
- 2in body lift from Wizardbilt.
- Llama 4x4 Extreme 4in suspension lift kit.
- Side exit exhaust.
- QT diff guards.
- Jackable sills.
- Bull bar.
- Brownchurch Roof rack.
- Snorkel.
- Electric fans.
- Light bar and spotlights.

Chapter 11
Technical specs

RANGE ROVER

Production
1970 to 1995

Length
176in (4470mm)
183in (4648mm) LSE

Width
70in (1778mm)

Height
Originally 1800mm (70.9in) but dropped
to 1780mm (70.1in) 1980 onwards

Wheelbase
100in (2540mm)
except LSE 2743mm (108.0in)

Fuel capacity
86.5L (22.9 US gal/19.0 imp gal)

Weight
1761kg (1970 2dr)
1972kg (1986 Vogue)
2016kg (1988 Turbo D)
2009kg (1992 Vogue SE)

Production years	Engine	Maximum power	Maximum torque	Fuel economy (mpg)	Top speed (mph)
1989-1996	3.9 V8i	Petrol 181bhp@4750rpm	231lb ft@3100rpm	12-18	110
1989-1994	2.5 200Tdi	111bhp@4000rpm	195lb ft@1800rpm	22-30	97
1994-1996	2.5 300Tdi	111bhp@4000rpm	195lb ft@1800rpm	22-30	97

Other engines:
3.5L V8 Carburettor 134hp
3.5L V8 Injection 155hp
4.2L V8 Injection 200hp
2.4L I4 VM Turbo diesel 112hp
2.5L I4 VM Turbo diesel 119hp

The long wheel base LSE was sold in the US as the County with the 3.9 V8. Exact figures for power vary by territory and emissions regulations.

VIN codes for 1989 to 1996
Example: **SALLHAMM3GA012345**

SALLHAMM3GA012345
Manufacturer code (Rover Group)

SAL**LH**AMM3GA012345
Range Rover

SALLH**A**MM3GA012345
Standard (100in) wheelbase
B = Long (108in) wheelbase

SALLHA**M**M3GA012345
Four-door body
B = Two-door body
A = Two-door commercial body

SALLHAM**M**3GA012345
3.9-litre V8 petrol engine
F = 2.5-litre 200Tdi diesel engine
N = 2.5-litre VM diesel engine
3 = 4.2-litre V8 petrol engine

SALLHAMM**3**GA012345
RHD with automatic gearbox
4 = LHD with automatic gearbox
7 = RHD with 5-speed manual gearbox
8 = LHD with 5-speed manual gearbox

SALLHAMM3**G**A012345
1990 model year
H = 1991
J = 1992
K = 1993
L = 1994
M = 1995
N = 1996

SALLHAMM3G**A**012345
Assembled at Solihull

SALLHAMM3GA**012345**
Serial number

DEFENDER

Production
1983 to 1990

Wheelbase
92.9in (2360mm) (90)
110in (2794mm) (110)
127in (3226mm) (127 and 130)

Length
144in (3658mm) (90 Pick up)
153in (3886mm) (2000s 90)
172in (4369mm) (110 Pick up)
182.3in (4630mm) (2000s 110)

183in (4648mm) (110 Hardtop)
174.7in (4437mm)
157.1in (3990mm) (1997-2000s 90)
160.5in (4077mm) (1990-94 90)
181.1in (4600mm) (1990s 110)
204in (5182mm) (130)

Width
70.5in (1791mm) (1990s)
70in (1778mm) (2000s 90)

Height
80in (2032mm) (2000s 90)

80.2in (2037mm) (1990s 90)
90.0in (2286mm) (110)

Weight
1630kg (early 90 soft top)
1695kg (early 90 hard top)
1815kg (early 110 hard top)
1759kg (2010 90 hard top)
1953kg (2010 110 hard top)
2050kg (2010 110 Station Wagon)
2137kg (2010 130 Double cab HCPU)

Production years	Engine	Maximum power	Maximum torque	Fuel economy (mpg)	Top speed (mph)
1983-1990	2.25 petrol	74bhp@4000rpm	120lb ft@2000rpm	18-23	70
1983-1990	2.5 petrol	83bhp@4000rpm	133lb ft@2000rpm	18-23	75
1983-1990	3.5 V8	114bhp@4000rpm	185lb ft@2500rpm	14-18	85
1983-1990	2.25 diesel	60bhp@4000rpm	103lb ft@1800rpm	20-25	75
1983-1990	2.5 diesel	67bhp@4000rpm	114lb ft@1800rpm	23-28	70
1986-1990	2.5 turbo diesel	85bhp@4000rpm	150lb ft@1800rpm	21-27	80
1991-1993	2.5 200Tdi	111bhp@4000rpm	195lb ft@1800rpm	22-28	80
1993-1998	2.5 300Tdi	111bhp@4000rpm	195lb ft@1800rpm	22-28	80
1999-2007	2.5 TD5	122bhp@4200rpm	221lb ft@1950rpm	22-29	85

Other engines:
3.5L 134bhp (100kW) V8 petrol
(1986–1993)
3.9L 182bhp (136kW) V8 petrol
2.4L 122bhp (91kW) I4 ZSD turbo diesel

VIN codes
Defender from 1984 to 1994
Example: **SALLDHAF7BA012345**

SALLDHAF7BA012345
Manufacturer code (Rover Group)

SAL**LD**HAF7BA012345
Defender

SALLD**H**AF7BA012345
110in wheelbase
K = 127in wheelbase (130)
R = 110in wheelbase
S = 110in wheelbase (military)
V = 90in wheelbase

SALLDH**A**F7BA012345
Truck cab with soft top or hard top body
B = Two-door Station Wagon (90)
E = Two-door Crew Cab (110 & 130)
F = Four-door Crew Cab (110 & 130)
H = High Capacity Pick Up (110)
M = Four-door Station Wagon (110)

SALLDHA**F**7BA012345
2.5-litre 200Tdi diesel engine

C = 2.5-litre diesel engine
D = 2.5-litre petrol engine
L = 3.5-litre V8 carburettor petrol engine

SALLDHAF**7**BA012345
RHD with 5-speed manual gearbox
8 = LHD with 5-speed manual gearbox

SALLDHAF7**B**A012345
1985-1987 model year
A = 1983-1984 (127 only)
E = 1998
F = 1989
G = 1990
H = 1991
J = 1992
K = 1993
L = 1994

SALLDHAF7B**A**012345
Assembled at Solihull
F= Shipped as KD for overseas assembly

SALLDHAF7BA**012345**
Serial number

Slight changes for 1994 to 1998
SALLD**H**AF7MA012345
Only H, K, and V (meanings the same)

SALLDH**A**F7MA012345
Only A and M (meanings the same)

SALLDHA**F**7MA012345
2.5-litre 300Tdi diesel engine
(1995-1996)
Y = 2.0-litre four-cylinder petrol engine
6 = 2.5-litre 300Tdi diesel engine
(1997 on)

SALLDHAF7**M**A012345
1995 model year
T = 1996
V = 1997
W = 1998

Slight changes for 1998 to 2010
SALLDHA**8**7MA012345
2.5-litre TD5 diesel engine, UK version
6 = 2.5-litre 300Tdi (special order RSA assembly)
7 = TD5 for outside UK/EEC/Australia/Japan
9 = TD5 for Australia/EEC/Japan

SALLDHA87**X**A012345
1999 model year
Y = 2000
1 = 2001, after that the number denotes the model year

DISCOVERY

Production
1989 to 1999

Wheelbase
100.0in (2540mm)

Length
178.7in (4539mm)

Width
70.6in (1793mm)

Height
77.4in (1966mm)

Weight
1882kg (V8 3dr),

1885kg (V8 5dr),
2008Kg (200Tdi 3dr),
2053Kg (200Tdi 5dr),
1979Kg (300 series V8 5dr),
1890kg (Mpi 3dr), 1925Kg (Mpi 5dr)

Production years	Engine	Maximum power	Maximum torque	Fuel economy (mpg)	Top speed (mph)
1989-1997	2.0 Mpi Petrol	134bhp@6000rpm	137lb ft@2500rpm	18-29	98
1989-1990	3.5 V8 Petrol	144bhp@5000rpm	192lb ft@2800rpm	14-20	95
1990-1993	3.5 V8i Petrol	165bhp@4750rpm	207lb ft@3200rpm	16-18	105
1995-1998	3.9 V8i Petrol	182bhp@4750rpm	231lb ft@3100rpm	13-27	106
1989-1994	2.5 200 Tdi	111bhp@4000rpm	195lb ft@1800rpm	23-32	92
1994-1998	2.5 300 Tdi	111bhp@4000rpm	195lb ft@1800rpm	23-33	92

The 300Tdi was also available with 129bhp on Auto gearbox models.

VIN codes
Example: **SALLJGBV3GA012345**

SALLJGBV3GA012345
Manufacturer code (Rover Group)

SAL**LJ**GBV3GA012345
Discovery

SALLJ**G**BV3GA012345
Standard (100in) wheelbase

SALLJGB**B**V3GA012345
Three-door body
M = Five-door body

SALLJGB**V**3GA012345
3.5-litre V8 carburettor petrol engine
F = 2.5-litre 200 or 300Tdi diesel engine
L = 3.5-litre V8 injected petrol engine
M = 3.9-litre V8 injected petrol engine
Y = 2.0-litre four-cylinder petrol engine

SALLJGBV**3**GA012345
RHD with automatic gearbox
4 = LHD with automatic gearbox
7 = RHD with 5-speed manual gearbox
8 = LHD with 5-speed manual gearbox

SALLJGBV3**G**A012345
1990 model year
H = 1991

J = 1992
K = 1993
L = 1994
M = 1995
T = 1996
V = 1997
W = 1998

SALLJGBV3G**A**012345
Assembled at Solihull
F = Shipped as KD for overseas assembly

SALLJGBV3GA**012345**
012345 Serial number

Chapter 12
Useful contacts

LAND ROVER & OFF-ROAD PREPARATION SPECIALISTS

Devon 4x4
Southlea Service Station
South Molton
Devon
EX36 3QU
UK
http://www.devon4x4.com
+44 (0) 1769 550900

Tomcat Motorsport
Old Wood
Skellingthorpe
Lincoln
LN6 5UA
http://www.tomcatmotorsport.co.uk/
01522 683733

Rakeway
Unit J Brookhouse Way
Brookhouse Industrial Estate
Cheadle
Stoke-on-Trent
Staffordshire
England
ST10 1SR
http://www.rakeway.co.uk/
01538 750500

Qt Services
Unit 11 B Miller Business Park
Station Road
Liskeard
PL14 4DA
http://www.qtservices.co.uk/partners/
+44 (0) 1579 349688

PARTS SUPPLIERS

Dunsfold Land Rover
Alfold Road
Dunsfold
Surrey
GU8 4NP
http://www.dunsfold.com/
tel +44 (0) 1483 200567

John Craddock Ltd
North Street
Bridgtown
Cannock
Staffordshire
WS11 0AZ
http://www.johncraddockltd.co.uk

Paddock Spares
The Showground
The Cliff
Matlock
Derbyshire
DE4 5EW
http://www.paddockspares.com

MM4x4
Droitwich Road
Martin Hussingtree
Worcester
WR3 8TE
http://www.mm-4x4.com/
+44 (0) 1905 451506

Rimmer Bros
Triumph House
Sleaford Road
Bracebridge Heath
Lincoln
LN4 2NA
http://www.rimmerbros.co.uk/
+44(0)1522 568000

ENGINES

RPi
Wayside Garage
Holt Road
Horsford
Norwich
Norfolk
NR10 3EE
United Kingdom
http://www.v8engines.com/
+44 (0)1603 891209

Real Steel
Unit 9, Tomo Industrial Estate
Packet Boat Lane
Cowley
Middlesex
UB8 2JP
http://www.realsteel.co.uk
01895 440505

TRANSMISSIONS

Ashcroft transmissions
Ashcroft Transmissions Ltd
Units 5 & 6
Stadium Estate
Cradock Rd
Luton
Beds
LU4 0JF
UK
http://www.ashcroft-transmissions.co.uk/
01582 496040

ELECTRONIC CONTROLS

Emerald (programmable engine ECU)
Unit 6
Norwich Road Industrial Estate
Watton
Norfolk
IP25 6DR
UK
http://www.emeraldm3d.com/
01953 889110

Nanocom
info@nanocom.it
support@nanocom.it
www.nanocom.it

CLUBS

AWDC
All Wheel Drive Club
PO Box 186
UCKFIELD
TN22 3YQ
http://awdc.co.uk/
01825 731875

Mud Club
http://www.mud-club.com/

There are superb clubs all over the world, far too many to list here, just try an internet search for 'Land Rover Club' in your area.

MUSEUMS

Heritage Motor Centre
Banbury Road
Gaydon
Warwickshire
CV35 0BJ
http://www.heritage-motor-centre.co.uk
01926 641188

The Dunsfold Collection
Alfold Road
Dunsfold
Surrey
GU8 4NP
http://www.dunsfoldcollection.co.uk/
01483 200567

FOLLOW LAND ROVER

Web site: http://www.landrover.com/
http://www.facebook.com/landrover.uk
http://www.landrover.co.uk
http://www.twitter.com/landrover_uk
http://www.youtube.com/landroveruk
http://www.flickr.com/photos/landroveruk

FOLLOW THE AUTHOR

http://twitter.com/RalphHosier

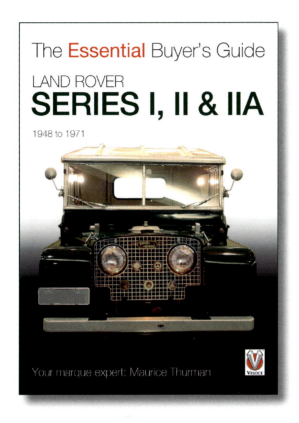

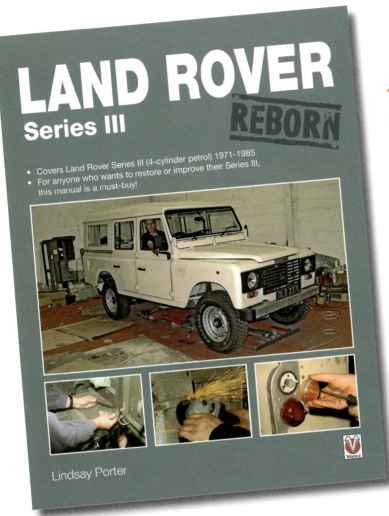

This manual is the most detailed package of information available for anyone thinking of restoring, rebuilding or improving a Series III Land Rover.

- Paperback
- 20.7x27cm
- £30.00/$59.95*
- 256 pages
- 1749 pictures!
- ISBN: 978-1-845843-47-2

We took a low-mileage, ex-military, unregistered Series III Land Rover, stripped it down to its bare bones, and then blended it with an original Series III Station Wagon in very poor condition. After stirring into the pot a selection of new and modified parts from a number of different sources, we ended up with the most immaculate and user-friendly Series III you could imagine.

Here's how you can restore or modify your own Series III, from suspension, brakes, and steering, to engine, transmission and body improvements. You want better seats? Galvanised chassis and bulkhead? Immaculately restored body and mechanical components? Developed from several years of articles in *Land Rover Monthly* magazine, this manual has all the answers.

Featuring advice on rebuilding the rear body tub, the bulkhead, Station Wagon side frames, and much more besides, this book is a must!

For more info on Veloce titles;
visit our website at www.veloce.co.uk • email: info@veloce.co.uk • Tel: +44(0)1305 260068
* prices subject to change, p&p extra

BRITPART
Suspension Products

Super Gaz Shock Absorbers

Part No.	Application	Lift	Fitment
DC5000	Discovery 2		Front
DC5000L	Discovery 2	50mm/2"	Front
DC5001	Discovery 2		Rear
DC5001L	Discovery 2	50mm/2"	Rear
DC5002	Defender/Discovery 1/ Range Rover Classic		Front
DC5002L	Defender/Discovery 1/ Range Rover Classic	50mm/2"	Front
DC5003	Defender/Discovery 1/Range Rover Classic		Rear
DC5003L	Defender/Discovery 1/ Range Rover Classic	50mm/2"	Rear
DC5004	Defender		Steering damper
DC5005	Range Rover Classic/Discovery 1/Series		Steering damper

> Over 30,000 springs and shock absorbers being used worldwide
> 24 month / 50,000 mile warranty on Super Gaz shocks*
> Dramatic improvement in ride & handling - in fact they are probably the single biggest improvement you can make to your Land Rover!
> Full range of Super Gaz shock absorber kits available - see web for full details

Cellular Dynamic Shock Absorbers

Part No.	Application	Lift	Fitment
DC6000	Defender/Discovery 1/Range Rover Classic		Front
DC6000L	Defender/Discovery 1/Range Rover Classic	50mm/2"	Front
DC6000LL	Defender/Discovery 1/Range Rover Classic	125mm/5"	Front
DC6001	Defender/Discovery 1/Range Rover Classic		Rear
DC6001L	Defender/Discovery 1/Range Rover Classic	50mm/2"	Rear
DC6001LL	Defender/Discovery 1/Range Rover Classic	125mm/5"	Rear
DC6002	Range Rover P38 - air suspension		Front
DC6003	Range Rover P38 - air suspension		Rear
DC6010	Discovery 2		Front
DC6011	Discovery 2		Rear
DC6004	Defender		Steering Damper
DC6005	Series/Discovery 1/Range Rover Classic		Steering Damper
DC6006	Range Rover P38		Steering Damper
DC6009	Discovery 2		Steering Damper

> Cellular technology tube
> Sintered 18mm rod
> Piston diameter 41mm
> Polyurethane bush
> Teflon piston with multi-lip seal
> Single piece eye ring
> Full range of heavy-duty Cellular Dynamic shock absorber kits available - see web for full details

Performance Britpart Springs

Part No.	Application	Fitment	Lift	Load
DA4201	Defender - 90 & 110 Discovery 1 Range Rover Classic	Front	25mm	25kg
DA4202	Defender - 90, 110 & 130 Discovery 1 Range Rover Classic	Front	40mm	50kg
DA4203	Defender - 90 Discovery 1 & 2 Range Rover Classic	Rear	40mm	Light
DA4204	Defender - 90 Discovery 1 Range Rover Classic	Rear	50mm	100kg
DA4205	Defender - 90 Discovery 1 & 2 Range Rover Classic	Rear	50mm	200kg
DA4206	Defender - 110	Rear	40mm	100kg
DA4208	Defender - 110 & 130	Rear	50mm	500kg
DA4199	Discovery 2	Front	40mm	20 - 50kg
DA4198	Discovery 2	Front	40mm	50 - 100kg
DA4197	Discovery 2	Rear	40mm	Medium

Britpart Air To Coil Spring Conversion Kits

DA5136	Discovery 2 - standard ride height	Rear kit
DA5007	Discovery 2 - 2" lift ride height - **heavy-duty** Ideal if winch is fitted	Front & rear kit
DA5008	Discovery 2 - 2" lift ride height	Front & rear kit
DA4136	Range Rover P38 - 1995 - 2002 Petrol models and diesel light duty	Front & rear kit
DA4136HD	Range Rover P38 - 1995 - 2002 Heavy-duty 1" lift including diesel models	Front & rear kit
DA4179	Range Rover Classic - no module	

For 30 years Britpart has been supplying quality parts and accessories for Land Rover users across the world and now we are very proud to announce that all* Britpart parts and accessories will be backed by an industry leading 24 month guarantee.

24 month Guarantee BRITPART

BRITPART
The quality parts for Land Rovers

For the full details -
www.britpart.com/suspension

* Terms and conditions apply. Part numbers are used for identification purposes only and do not imply or indicate the identity of the manufacturer. E&OE. Products available from your local Britpart stockist.

Index